SPY in the SKY

By EDWARD CLACK

First published in 1992

ISBN 0 9520073 0 4

High Flight

Oh! I have slipped the surly bonds of Earth
And dance the skies on laughter-silvered wings
Sunward I've climbed, and joined the tumbling mirth
Of sun-spilt clouds, and done a hundred things
You have not dreamed of, wheeled and soared and swung
High in the sunlit silence. Hov'ring there,
I've chased the shouting wind along, and flung
My eager craft through footless halls of air...
Up, up the long, delirious blue
I've topped the wind-swept heights with easy grace,
Where never lark, or even eagle flew —
And while the silent, lifting mind I've trod
The high untrespassed sanctity of space,
Put out my hand and touched the Face of God.

John Gillespie Magee Jnr., RCAF, 1941

Pilot Officer Magee composed this beautiful poem on 3rd September, 1941, after his first trip in a Spitfire. Aged 19, he was killed in a mid-air collision on 11th December, 1941.

The Swiss Alps from flight level 330 (approx. 33,000 feet)

A MkVIII Magic Carpet, on loan from the Caliph of Baghdad.
Adapted for photo reconnaissance, here on patrol over the Shatt-al-Arab.

INTRODUCTION

It has been said that often a pilot learns to fly in spite of his instructor not because of him, so it was with me! Only fifteen when the last war started, like most boys of my age I was anxious to join the RAF and of course nothing but Spitfires to fly would be sufficient. I joined the Air Training Corps as soon as it was formed and had my first and very memorable flight with them, in a De Havilland Rapide out of Hendon in North London, alas no longer an airfield but home to the RAF Museum. At seventeen and a quarter, the earliest age at which one could volunteer, I passed the medical and all the aptitude tests for RAF aircrew. However, in October when I was called up, to my bitter disappointment, pilots were no longer being recruited and the officer, knowing of my interest in photography, offered me the role of reconnaissance photographer.
I went to the RAF school of photography at Blackpool, spent a short time at RAF Station Leconfield in Lincolnshire, then in May 1943 sailed on a vast convoy out of Greenock for the war in North Africa. The journey with its stops, one for six weeks in Durban which was wonderful, took a long time and when we eventually docked in Egypt, Alamain had been and the war in North Africa was over.
With six others I was posted to RAF Habbaniyah near Baghdad in Iraq where after an interesting journey across the Sinai, through Palestine (now Israel), The Lebanon to Damascus in Syria where I boarded a desert bus to Baghdad.
There I spent the next four years, first with Air Headquarters then with a Photographic recognisance unit flying many photographic sorties in may types of aircraft. They included a Vicker Vallencia, Blenheim Walrus, and I had one very memorable flight in the 'C' class flying boat 'Cleopatra', to name but a few.
There in the deserts of Iraq, Arabia the Emirates and Persia my love of flying and of photography were consolidated and I was first called 'The Spy in the Sky'.
Demobbed in 1947, the opportunity to fly did not occur again until 1956, when I gained my Private Pilot's Licence at Stapleford aerodrome with the Herts and Essex Aero Club. At first I did not enjoy my flying training, the instructor was both aggressive and loud but the desire to achieve the licence was strong, so I persisted in spite of him. Later, Ron Jones became Chief Flying Instructor at Stapleford. Ron was a big man with a heart to match, flying became again, what it should have been all along, a delight. I eventually gained my licence, Ron a little later went to British Air Ferries where he finished up Chief Pilot, Ron sadly died a few years ago, and I owe him much. Later I gained my instructor's rating, a commercial pilot's licence with instrument rating, and made a vow that any one entering a club I was associated with would have a warm greeting, and as well as teaching the skills of flying I would do my best to ensure that anybody sharing a flight with me would enjoy the experience of flying.

Later I had the opportunity to fly full time, when at Southend Airport, I took up the post of Chief Flying Instructor with Southend Light Aviation Centre on March 3rd 1968, and it was the twenty years at Southend in that role which were my most rewarding. During the period, I myself flew some 15,000 hours and supervised about 100,000 hours. About 400 of the student pilots were RAF cadets, 1000 various flying instructor courses were completed. Many of those pilots are now flying airliners all over the world, and not to be forgotten, those many who flew just for the love of it. I am very proud that during all that flying not one person was so much as scratched as a result. This was due not only to my supervision but to the dedicated flying instructors who worked with me, to Mary Dunbar and my daughter Deborah both of whom took care of the mass of administration, to the engineers who serviced the aircraft and the ground staff at Southend who refuelled them. Not to be forgotten are those people who, to pilots, are just 'voices' on the R.T. (Radio Telephony) the controllers who have assisted us safely down in all weathers to something like a quarter of a million safe landings.

So it was, after completing some advanced flying training with Clive Simpson, now captain with Titan Airways in command of a Shorts 330 I received the following:-

To Edward,

Have a lovely time: keep taking those beautiful aerial photographs:
and thankyou for all your help and kindness with my flying instruction;
and for giving me a greater appreciation of the wonderful world as seen from the air.

Clive Simpson, Braintree, Essex.

Of course many of these beautiful places I see from above, make superb photographs, especially in the changing seasons, when seen from the more prosaic viewpoint at ground level.

Very often I follow some air photography with a visit to the location by road. Once off the main roads motoring can often be a pleasure again, with little traffic and quiet picturesque villages to pass through and so the air and ground photography complement each other as you will find in this book.

Edward Clack

DEDICATION

...so to all those; and to everyone who has shared an aircraft with me in the past.

To those who will fly with me in the future and enjoy 'The Beauty of Flight'

and to those, who perhaps cannot fly, but will still be able to explore our wonderful countryside and magnificent places.

THIS BOOK IS DEDICATED

Edward Clack

Contents

Published by

Air and ground photography by Edward Clack

Paintings by Ronald Slade

Reconstructing the past—Paintings by Peter Froste

The author wishes to thank Philip Crummy, director of the Colchester Archaeological Trust for his help in researching The Royal Graves (Hidden Essex)

Designed and produced by Grant Graphics

A final check of the map before getting airborne. Journalist Janet Knight and chief instructor Derek Bidwell.

Try a Trial Flying Lesson

Most of the flying clubs in Essex are able to offer trial flying lessons, either booked directly, or in the form of a gift when a gift voucher is available to be redeemed at a convenient time. And what a wonderful gift! An experience the memory of which will last a lifetime.

What then is a trial flying lesson?

The trial flying lesson is a short flight undertaken with a pilot who is also a flying instructor; it will last about twenty five to thirty minutes. During the flight the 'student pilot' will be given the opportunity to take control of the aircraft, and this usually surprises them!

Most recipients of a 'Trial Flying Lesson Gift Voucher' are more than a little overcome at first; then, on getting over the initial shock they can't make the telephone call quickly enough to book the flight. The call will confirm a mutually convenient time and a request to attend half an hour early for a 'pre-flight briefing' just like a full flying lesson! Even if your family have not thought to make such a gift you can still call the flying club and book your own 'Trial Flying Lesson'. It is best to enjoy a flight on a nice day, so if the weather is poor on the day you have booked, a change of date can be usually made without charge.

Reporting at the Flying Club will, for most people, be tinged with a little apprehension and, this is understandable. You will be in a machine you don't understand, entering an environment which is unfamiliar, with a flying instructor whose skills are unknown.

The Flying Instructor

First then a little about the flying instructor who will initiate you into the wonders of flying. It is interesting to note that however experienced a pilot may be he or she is not allowed to give instruction in flying without having first completed a flying instructors' course. This is because the skills required to teach flying are very different from those needed to fly a 'Jumbo Jet' across the Atlantic. Your instructor will be a person with considerable flying experience who has also undertaken a course in how to teach flying and have passed a test with an instructor/examiner appointed by the Civil Aviation Authority, for that purpose. He will be tested on his ability to fly the aircraft, to give instruction in flying and teach the associated classrooom subjects, navigation, meteorology, aviation law, etc. The test has to be retaken periodically to ensure standards are maintained. My role in flying now is mainly concerned with conducting flying instructors' courses. My experience in giving flying instruction is considerable, yet even so I had to be tested and appointed to train other pilots to become flying instructors. And again, I have to be retested in that role periodically.

In an aircraft the captain normally occupies the left hand seat, so when I am training a flying instructor because I have to pretend to be a student pilot I am usually in that seat. I demonstrate to my student instructor how to present a flying lesson; then it is my turn to 'be a student pilot'. My student instructor then has to 'teach me to fly'. I can make all the mistakes a trainee pilot can make together with a few more, and I expect my student instructor to correct me; of course sometimes I complete my exercises perfectly and then I look for some praise. After completing the course to gain an instructors' rating and passing a test both in flying and knowledge of the associated 'ground' subjects the pilot can then start to put his new-found skills to use and enjoy teaching someone to fly. So the instructor is well skilled in that roll and able to give the 'trial lesson' student considerable participation in the control of the aircraft from the beginning.

Pre-flight briefing in classroom.

A final check of the weather before flying; a most important duty.

The Briefing

On meeting your instructor you will find him/her very relaxed and apart from an introduction to the skills of handling the aircraft you will be helped to enjoy the flight as he does. You will be given a little talk, we call it a 'pre-flight briefing', with the aid of a wallboard and model aircraft, then taken to the aircraft. It is likely to be a high wing Cessna 150/152 or a Piper Cherokee. You will be very safe in the hands of your well trained very experienced flying instructor.

About the Aircraft

Aircraft have of course to be built to very stringent standards and subjected to many tests before they are considered fit to be produced, then tested individually before being granted a C. of A. *(Certificate of Airworthiness).* In this country the C.A.A. *(Civil Aviation Authority)* has to be satisfied that all aircraft are fit to be flown. For this purpose an in-depth inspection together with flight tests are carried out before the granting of a C. of A. Inspections and tests which are repeated each three years before the renewal of the aircraft's certificate. In addition the aircraft is required to have frequent periodical inspections conducted by a licensed engineer, while the pilot, before each flight makes a pre-flight check. All faults found, except the most minor, for instance a light not working for a day flight, have to be rectified before the aircraft flies again.

The Aircraft Engine

One of the most common causes of failure in a car is the battery. An aircraft is not dependent on the battery for the running of the engine. The ignition system generates its own power, and to be doubly safe there are two completely independent ignition systems, both of which are tested before each flight. The flight is conducted with both ignition systems working, but the aircraft is capable of flying on either one. In the Cessna Aircraft the fuel is contained in the high wing above the engine and so is fed to the engine by gravity, there being no need for a fuel pump.

However, in a low wing aircraft, the fuel is still contained in the wings which are below the engine and the fuel has to be fed by pump. There are two pumps, one mechanical, which is driven by the engine and the other electrical, which can be switched as required. Both pumps are tested individually before flight.

The engine has a limited 'life' and the hours it runs have to be carefully accounted. When the alloted hours are completed the engine has to be removed and, before re-use, overhauled by an approved engine overhaul organisation. An exchange re-certified engine can be, and usually is, installed in the aircraft instead of waiting for an overhaul to be completed.

So, as far as it is possible all the likely problems have been eliminated and as a consequence the aircraft is very safe and I am pleased to say mechanical failure is a very rare occurence.

Janet relaxes in the pilot's seat in Cherokee 'Alpha Romeo' just before take-off.

Janet at the controls, 'Alpha Romeo' is over the River Blackwater.

The Flight

After the pre-flight briefing you will be taken to the aircraft and see the 'walk-round', the pre-flight inspection a pilot completes before every flight. Then you will be made comfortable in the left seat (the captain's position) there you will be shown the aircraft controls which are completely dual, the engine controls and flight instruments. After starting the engine taxi clearance will be given to the holding point, the holding point is just before the runway where the engine will be 'run-up', that is, checked, and the aircraft prepared for take-off.

Take-off clearance is given by A.T.C. (air traffic control) and acknowledged by your instructor who then says to you "follow me on the controls". Together you apply full power, keeping the Cessna straight on the runway the aircraft accelerates to 20, 30, 40, 55mph then you ease back on the control column and the aircraft becomes airborne. You will climb straight ahead to six hundred feet then make a left turn towards the river, one thousand feet and now straight and level the instructor says "you have control" and for the first time the aircraft responds to your control inputs.

Climbing, turning, descending, twenty minutes goes like a flash, then there ahead is the runway, you will need a little help with the landing and you respond to "follow me on the controls" and lightly take the controls with the instructor still flying the aircraft. As the power is eased off, the ground comes up towards the aircraft, the nose gently rises as the instructor moves the control column back, airspeed decays, the control column comes further back, the nose rises a little higher, then with a gentle 'swish' the wheels touch the runway. Back on the ground the aircraft is kept straight until the speed is reduced to a safe taxiing pace, and following the controller's instruction the aircraft is moved to its parking space by the flying club and shutdown. Your trial lesson is complete.

Your instructor will have been at pains to make sure you have enjoyed both the flight and the sights which are to be seen, together with the experience of flying an aircraft for the very first time. Most people are thrilled by their flight and usually express surprise at the amount of control they are given. So what are the dangers. There is but one I know. Flying in a light aircraft is addictive, you will want to do it again and again.

Many I know who started with a 'trial lesson' are now flying great airliners all over the world. One young lady who came to me in response to a dare was so taken with flying she went on to gain her private pilot's licence then the instructors' rating and on to the commercial flying licence when she flew Carvairs out of Southend. Now Captain Wendy Crick is an examiner with the Civil Aviation Flying Unit, making sure commercial pilots achieve and maintain their standards.

The Trial Flying Lesson; some impressions!

By Janet Knight

Clambering into the light aircraft's tiny cockpit, although presented with a mass of instruments and levers, I felt confident that my first flying lesson would be a cinch, high anxiety was the last thing on my mind. An hour later, after an exhilarating experience and enjoying vistas of the River Blackwater and Essex on a beautiful clear day, I was not sure if my flying career had taken a 'nose dive' or would in the future soar heavenwards.

Free from vertigo, panic attacks, claustrophobia and a myriad of other symptoms, I had been looking forward to playing the role of pilot in my first trial flying lesson; or so I thought.

Within a few seconds of having the seat belt adjusted and being made comfortable in the pilot's position in Piper Cherokee 'Alpha Romeo' we were moving towards Southend's Runway '24'. Fears of a sudden engine failure were alleviated as Chief Flying Instructor Derek Bidwell explained; as he completed the engine and aircraft pre-take-off checks, about the safety features which render power failures as almost an impossibility.

Within a few seconds of getting clearance to enter the runway and take-off, following Derek on the controls, we slowly opened the throttle, accelerated, and at 70mph eased the control column back and we were airborne.

Whether in a Boeing 747 or a simple Piper Cherokee, the amazing moment of lift-off never ceases to give me an adrenalin fuelled 'kick-start', a moment even more exhilarating when I considered our light aircraft, which looked as fragile as an Airfix model.

Having levelled at one thousand feet, the speed now 130mph, we turned towards Bradwell, now it was my turn; Derek said, "You have control", as I tentatively took the control column, the aircraft, for the first time, responded to my control inputs.

"Find the line on the horizon and follow it, my tutor told me, "while also keeping an eye on the wings to check they remain level". All that sounded pretty simple but I was not prepared for the sensitivity of the control column. Worse were the bumps which seemed to bounce the plane up and down by several feet, to be overcome. This, I was assured, was normal on a bright sunny day; being nothing more sinsiter than temperature changes.

By moving the control column a fraction, the nose would either rise or dive dramatically; and, I thought, one false move and I will perform an unintentional 'aeronautical stunt' like 'looping the loop'. But, I had no cause for fear for my instructor was there; close to the dual controls.

Having mastered the art of flying in a reasonably straight line, I was now instructed to try a turn or two. This simply involved gently guiding the column left or right like a car steering wheel, this caused the aircraft to bank in that direction. As we began to bank left my stomach lurched to the right. Suddenly I was facing the ground and felt as though I was about to tumble out of the aircraft, however the aircraft righted as I moved the control column the other way to prevent the impending sensation of death. "I have control", said Derek, and a huge sense of relief washed over me as my instructor joined me back on the dual controls. "How did that feel?", he asked, "Wonderful", I replied, "but I was not prepared for how sensitive the aircraft is to the controls". Safely back under his guidance I then began to appreciate that only small, smooth gentle movements of the controls were all that was needed to make 'Alpha Romeo' respond. So, until I have a few more lessons, for the time being the thrill experienced by such sky-bound heroes as Biggles will have to elude me.

Then came a spell of formation flying when the Echo's own 'Spy in the Sky' cameraman, Edward Clack, in Cessna 'Lima Whiskey' joined us.

Edward, who is also an accomplished pilot and instructor needed some flying lesson pictures for his new book.

Flying in tandem is a highly skillful manoeuvre which involves travelling at low speed, giving the impression that the plane is about to stall. After series of watching me watching you type shots were completed it was time to venture home.

Edward in the Cessna broke away, and I sat back as my instructor banked to the right for a sharp 90 degree turn, which would take us back to base. This did not bother me as I had the security of knowing we were in good hands.

I shared the flying on the return leg which took us over North East Essex. It had been a crystal clear day for my first flying lesson, which, when finished, although it had been an hour, felt as though it had lasted about 10 minutes.

Back at Seawing Flying Club, I was given heart when Derek explained that some of the adverse sensations I had experienced were not uncommon in first time pilots and with further flying would soon disappear.

Then I was presented with a certificate and a log book, the log book recording my first flying lesson and the first step to a Pilot's licence.

Janet Knight is a reporter with the Evening Echo Newspaper. Perhaps now she has had a taste of flying and has seen Essex in all its richness from the air it will give her a new insight into her profession, and occasionally supplement the various attributes of our wonderful county when explored from the ground with observations gained from a light aircraft.

'A January Evening' looking across The Thames Estuary from the Esplanade Leigh-on-Sea.

Essex—Rich and Beautiful

It has often been said that Essex is flat and uninteresting, one cynic even said, "It is slightly hilly but still uninteresting". These people must have moved about Essex without opening their eyes and ears for there is much to be enjoyed, both in what has remained of the past, what is happening now, and our rich abundance of wildlife. Especially the thousands of wildfowl and waders who inhabit our lonely marshes.

Tilbury Fort. A complete example of 17th Century military architecture.

Many people equate Essex with the sprawl of ugly development which extends along our southern border, the River Thames. Yet every so often, set between the industrial developments is a fragment of our heritage. Tilbury Fort lies between the power station and the docks. In the care of English Heritage, Tilbury Fort is a magnificent example of 18th century military architecture. It still dominates the river guarding the river approach to London. The fort was never attacked although its anti aircraft guns shot down a Zeppelin during World War One. The most bloody incident occured there in 1776 during an Essex v Kent cricket match; an Essex cricketer was killed, an elderly invalid bayoneted and the sergeant of the guard shot dead.

'Sunset and Evening Star'. The River Thames by Tilbury.

Tilbury Fort — The Landgate. Built in 1716. Painting by Ron Slade.

H.M.S. Britannia' with the Queen Mother on board sailing past Tilbury on a misty morning. On the occasion of the Queen Mother's 90th Birthday.

The Ocean Terminal Tilbury. Here the new twin hulled cruise liner 'Radisson Diamond' is waiting to embark passengers and start its maiden cruise, the other ship is the'KapeΛnr'.

Here a 'tall ship' passes on its way to London and the start of the last 'Tall Ships Race' to start from our capital.

Tilbury Fort was built on the site of a Tudor block house and it was there or nearby that Queen Elizabeth I reviewed her troops before the armada and made her famous speech.

> *"I am come amongst you , as you see, at this time, not for my recreation and disport, but being resolved, in the midst and heat of the battle, to live or die amongst you all...I know I have the body of a weak and feeble woman, but I have the heart and stomach of a King, and a King of England too, and think foul scorn that Parma or Spain, or any Prince of Europe should dare to invade the borders of my realm..."*

Now the area is dominated by the Queen Elizabeth II Bridge. While inland is the new and vast Lakeside Retail Park.

The Thames Bridge. The day the two spans joined, June 11th 1991.

'The Queen Elizabeth II Bridge'. The day the bridge was opened by Her Majesty The Queen, October 30th 1991.

'Lakeside' Thurrock.

'Stubbers Walled Garden', Ockendon near Upminster. Note the Crinkle-Crankle wall, walls were built in this form both to make them stronger and to provide a larger area to grow plants against. This walled garden which has its origins in Tudor times is being restored by the 'Friends of Stubbers'. In the early 17th century, William Coys established at Stubbers one of the earliest plant collections. John Goodyer made lists of the plants there between 1617 and 1622, he named 324 plants an this list is probably the earliest known of English plants using Latin names.

'Upminster Windmill'. A fine example of a smock mill, so called because the body of the mill resembles a millers smock. Visitors can see this mill working at certain times.

Maplin Sands

This island on Maplin Sands was destined to grow into a vast airport, but then abandoned.

Close up of pipe through which was pumped water and gravel. The water flowed away and the gravel was pushed by bulldozers to form the island.

The eastern border of Essex where it meets the Thames at Shoeburyness is the lonely and beautiful Maplin Sands, used now as a firing range by the Ministry of Defence. We have all been spared the great airport which was planned to be built there. In 1976 a small island was created, the start of what was to be London's third airport, then the plans were abandoned. The island was oblong then, now the tides have made it crescent shaped. You will be pleased to know that it is being used for its original purpose, flying! When I last flew over it, thousands or sea birds and wildfowl had made it their home.

The island now. Tides have changed its shape, while waders and seabirds have made it their home.

'Stow Maries' WWI Aerodrome near Maldon. Now used by an aeromodel club. Here we see the buildings and countryside much as those First World War pilots must have done.

Essex with its close proximity to the continent was used a base for the military aircraft of both the world wars and the countryside is dotted with the remnants of these once very active bases.

One of the most interesting are the remnants of a first World War aerodrome at Flambirds Farm near the village of Stow Maries. Here the buildings used by the very young men who flew the fighters in that era can still be seen and I am sure that by walking amongst those buildings one would feel the ghosts of that period; as I sometimes do when I fly over it. Stow Maries village hall also has some memorabilia of that time and the 'airfield', like Maplin is still used for flying; a model aeroplane club now uses it.

Maldon and the River Blackwater

One of my favourite places is the River Blackwater. At the western end of the broad estuary lies the town of Maldon, always interesting but especially so from above. Hythe Quay usually has five or six colourful and lovingly restored Thames Barges tied up, and behind the quay on the hill, stands the church of St. Mary The Virgin, parts of which date from Norman times.

Unlike the River Thames the River Blackwater is largely unspoilt, both banks looking much as they have done for centuries. Here and there the remnants of a decoy pond can be seen and a few isolated villages edge the shore. Marinas are a new feature of some of the villages most crammed with boats when the owners are not out enjoying this quiet river, its tributaries and teaming wildlife.

Maldon, with the sails of Thames Barges drying on Hythe Quay.

Maldon and St. Mary's Church, sometimes called the fishermans church, with Thames Barges tied up on Hythe Quay.

Thames Barges on the River Blackwater.

Tollesbury Marina, on the River Blackwater.

The Bradwell Peninsular

The Bradwell Peninsular, taken in the springtime, the yellow fields are oil seed rape.

At the south eastern end of the River Blackwater where it meets the sea, is the Bradwell peninsular. It seems strange that here is situated one of Britain's most modern buildings, the vast nuclear power station, and the tiny little Saxon church of St. Peter's On The Wall, one of our most ancient buildings. Behind the power station is an aerodrome of WWII from which twin engined fighters roared into the air to intercept the raiders from Germany as they approached over the North Sea. The village of Bradwell is interesting, dominated as it is by the Parish Church of St. Thomas. However, I think it is the two features in the churchyard wall which are amongst the most fascinating. Close by the gate, which leads through the churchyard to the porch and church entrance are 'mounting steps'. Deep hollows have been worn in the steps as Ladies, in the Victorian period, climbed the steps to mount their horses, which were tethered to the iron post which still exists. At the other end of the wall close by some cottages is a Georgian 'lock-up' with the shackles of the whipping post still on the door pillar. Where unruly chaps from the village, perhaps having taken too much ale would be 'popped' overnight to sober up.

Bradwell-Juxta-Mare, The Church of St. Thomas the Apostle. At the end of the wall can be seen the Georgian village 'Lock-up'.

The Church of St. Thomas the Apostle. 'The Mounting Steps'. Painting by Ron Slade.

The Church of St. Thomas the Apostle. The Georgian village 'Lock-up'. Painting by Ron Slade.

The Saxon Church of 'St. Peter's-On-The-Wall'. Inset: Pilgrims on the old Roman road, July, 1992.

St. Peter's On The Wall

One of the oldest buildings still in use is the lonely little church by the Dengie Flats called St. Peter's On The Wall. When the Saxon Bishop St. Cedd sailed from Lindisfarne and landed in Essex much of the great 'Roman Fort of the Saxon Shore', Othona, was still standing; it must have been very like Housesteads *(a well preserved example of a Roman Fort on Hadrian's Wall in Northumberland).*

The year was 654 AD, when St. Cedd and his small party ran their boat ashore; by then the fort had been deserted. So with materials from the Roman buildings the Saxon Bishop and his followers built their little chapel astride the outer wall of the fort. Little now remains of 'Othona' the Roman Fort, apart from some stone, brick and tile which can be seen in the chapel wall, a 'crop-mark' *(see Hidden Essex)* through the adjacent field, some foundations beneath the soil, together with the name 'St. Peter's On The Wall'.

Housesteads, the best preserved Roman Fort in Britain. St. Cedd probably saw Othona like this when he arrived at Bradwell in 654 AD.

Abberton Reservoir

Abberton Reservoir lies just to the south of Colchester, it is so vast it is like an inland sea. Even now the waters are much depleted but nothing like as bad as they were after the long hot summer of 1989. The reservoir is a host to thousands of wildfowl, waders, swans and other birds who make it their home all the year round. In winter, when the migration flocks fly in is a good time to visit and the two causeways which cross the water are good places to view but, even better, is the Essex Wildlife Trust Centre and Observatory.

Abberton Reservoir, at the end of September 1989, after the worst of the drought. South of Colchester.

Colchester

Colchester was once the Roman Garrison town and the town is still a garrison today. Every other year a military tattoo is staged which must be one of the finest anywhere. An evening under the stars enjoying the spectacle and the splendid music is breathtaking. To the south of the town a large stretch of the Roman Wall survives together with the remains of the main Roman southern gate 'The Balkern Gate'. A book could be written on Colchester and its many interesting features but I will mention just two more. There is a massive castle keep which is where the last siege between the armies of the Civil War took place. Not too far away stands the imposing remains of St. Botolph's Priory. The remnants of this once magnificent building are tucked away behind one of Colchester's busiest streets. The impressive remains standing in tranquil grounds offer both a refuge from the bustle of today and place to contemplate a less secular past.

Colchester, with the Roman Town wall and Balkerne Gate in Foreground.

A scene from the Colchester Tattoo, 1990.

Colchester Castle.

St. Botolph's Priory Ruins, together with St. Botolph's Church which dates from 1838.

St. Botolph's Priory, as it might have looked in the 12-13th century. Painting Peter Froste.

Chappel Viaduct. Built in Victorian times to span the valley of the River Stour at Chappel. This railway viaduct caused great controversey when it was built due to its impact on the countryside. Now it remains an imposing monument to that era.

Colchester Zoo, Stanway Hall Park. The elephants can be seen in the ring.

St. Osyth

St. Osyth Priory.

Tranquility is also the dominant feature of St. Osyth, a village between Brightlingsea and Clacton. The Priory of St. Osyth is best seen from above when bathed in the light of a late soft afternoon sun. The fabulous gate house of St. Osyth is said to be the finest remaining monastic building in europe.

The origin of the name St. Osyth is part of the romance of Essex. Osyth was the daughter of Frithewald and Walburga, King and Queen of East Anglia who were the first rulers of East Anglia to adopt Christianity. Their daughter Osyth learned to love the new religion too, and also helped others to embrace Christianity. As soon as she was old enough she was betrothed to Sighere, son of the first Christian King of Essex, Sebert. The festivities were great but, in their midst, a stag went by and off went the bridegroom in pursuit. When Sighere returned to the feast, Osyth had already fled to the nearby nunnery. Sighere gave his wife of a few hours the village of Chich where Osyth founded a nunnery and gave the village her name.

Years later the Danes sailed up the River Colne on a raid, burned the church and nunnery and captured Osyth. Saintly Osyth would not bow to the Danes 'gods' and she was beheaded.

Legend has it that where she fell a fountain gushed forth; later Osyth was cannonised and today we remember her in the name of the village and the beautiful priory nearby.

The Port of Harwich. Inset The Redoubt, a defence built against the threat from Napoleon.

Harwich

The North East corner of Essex where the River Stour joins the sea is Harwich the Essex Gateway to the Continent. Still a busy port, and set amongst some modern houses and garden allotments is Harwich Redoubt a great Napoleonic defensive work. Nearby, tucked in between the ancient narrow streets of the old town is the oldest lighthouse in Essex.

Flatford Mill and the River Stour. Scene of many paintings by Constable.

The broad River Stour is again very unspoilt with wide expanses of marshes inhabited with the wildfowl which find their food amongst the shallows. At Manningtree the river narrows to little more than a stream and a short way inland the river flows through 'Constable Country' although Flatford Mill on the north bank of the Stour is just in Suffolk, since the painter John Constable was an Essex man, I still tend to think of Flatford Mill, where his father worked and John painted many of his masterpieces, as part of Essex.

A little further west and south of the river of Dedham. It was there that Constable lived.

From the 15th to 17th centuries, Dedham gained its prosperity from the wool trade, it was then the massive church was built by one of the villages' princely wool merchants. This year (1992) is the 500th anniversay of the church, and event to be celebrated with much activity. Within the church a pathetic reminder of our maritime heritage is the cover of the ancient font. It is made of oak from timbers recovered from the Royal George, a great warship, which in 1782 'turned turtle' and sank just off Portsmouth, taking with it about eight hundred men. Of this tragic event Cowper wrote:

> *Her timbers yet are sound,*
> *And she may float again,*
> *Full charged with England's*
> *thunder,*
> *And plough the distant main...*

The Royal George did not sail again!

The ancient font with the oaken cover made from wood recovered from H.M.S. Royal Oak.

The village of Dedham and the Parish Church of St. Mary the Virgin.

Marks Tey and Coggeshall

Following the Roman Road west from Marks Tey, Stane Street passes through Coggeshall a small quaint town with the now narrow river Blackwater flowing past to the south. There are 99 monuments scheduled there by the government. The Paycocke's house is supreme amongst the other 'gems' of richly ornamented houses of the Tudor Period. Coggeshall also owes its prosperity to the wool trade and like Dedham, the magnificent church was built at the height of that wealth. Perhaps one should say rebuilt for in with the flint rubble of the walls are Roman bricks and tiles which suggest it was fashioned from material from an earlier building. Crossing the River Blackwater by a brick bridge some 700 years old we come to a perfect little chapel of the 13th century. It owes its survival at the time of the dissolution to the fact that it was used as a barn. Dedicated to St. Nicholas, the patron saint of travellers, it stood at the gate of the monastery which was destroyed. The little church is famous amongst other things for 'thin pick bricks' forming arches especially round the windows and doors. These bricks are thought to be the earliest known in England since Roman times, and were probably made at Tylkell in north Essex. In this small chapel there is still a consecration cross marking the place where the Bishop placed his hand on the wall during its consecration some 700 years ago.

Many of the buildings in Coggeshall were fashioned from timber frames built of oaks which were abundant in the forests of Essex.

Above: *Coggeshall, standing on Stane Street, the Roman military road.*

Left: *Dedicated to St. Nicholas the patron saint of travellers this delightful 13th century chapel, which stood at the gate, is all that remains of the great monastery. It owes its survival due to the fact that it looked like a barn, of the rest, not a stone remains.*

Cressing Temple

Not too far from Stane Street near Braintree, is the magnificent site of Cressing Temple. Here a group of timber framed buildings are dominated by the wheat and barley barns.

Set in delightful unspoilt countryside, the manor of Cressing was granted to the Knights Templar 800 years ago, there they lived until they were suppressed. Cressing Temple was sacked during the peasants revolt in 1381 and later came to an end in the dissolution of the Monastries during the reign of Henry VIII. However, the great barns, built of Essex oaks held together with wooden pegs have survived from the 14th century, and even the hurricane of 1987 did little damage.

The great wheat and barley barns, Cressing Temple.

Audley End.

Audley End

At the north western border of Essex stands the noblest house in the county, Audley End. this magnificent building stands in a great park just north of Saffron Walden and through the park runs the River Cam.

There on the site of an abbey the Lord Treasurer built a great palace which at the time rivalled the finest in the land. It is said that James I, when he first saw it before completion remarked, "It is too much for a King' but it might do very well for a Lord Treasurer".

Charles II bought the house and it remained a royal palace until William II sold it back to the Suffolks who soon found it too expensive to maintain.

Three sides of the great quadrangle were demolished leaving the west front, the magnificent building we see today. Audley End is a treasure house set in a beautiful park with grounds hardly equalled anywhere. Audley Park is a place of tranquility with a number of classical buildings set on the high points, a Round Temple designed by Robert Adam, supported by many pillars the Temple of Concord, still remaining are the stables with delightful work of the tudor period.

Thaxted

Moving south, the spire of the great church dominating the countryside for miles around beckons us to Thaxted. The church which is probably the most magnificent in all Essex was begun in 1340 and is dedicated to St. John the Baptist, St. Mary and St. Lawrence, the latter the patron saint of cutlers. It was the cutlers and wool merchants who made Thaxted prosperous in the Middle Ages, a prosperity which we can still see in the buildings remaining today. For 500 years the Guildhall has dominated the broad market street, a wonderful example of a timber framed building, in which Essex abounds, created by skilled joiners with oak from the forests which in those days covered much of Essex.

Thaxted, the timber framed Guild Hall can be seen centre.

Epping Forest and High Beech

Thanks to the foresight of our Victorian ancestors a large tract of the ancient woodland remains, Epping Forest.

The countryside must have been more open in Roman times for not too far from Epping town in the midst of the forest is the remains of an iron age camp.

The camp covers 12 acres and the earth rampart and the ditch can still be seen in the forest, some say that it was the place of Boadicea's last fight with the Roman legions. Now covered with dense forest Amesbury Banks does not show well from above. But I was flying above the forest one bright winter's day when I saw a spire, bathed in soft winter sunshine, the evergreen in the churchyard was surrounded by the stark bare trunks of the noble beech wood. It was the Church of the Holy Innocents at High Beech. It was the beauty of the place which attracted Tennyson the greatest poet of the Victorian era to come here to live and work. Tennyson loved to walk the forest paths, to rest in the forest glades and in winter to skate on the pond. Here, walking back home one winters day, past the lofty spire of the Church of the Holy Innocents he heard the bells of Waltham Abbey Ringing out across the forest, and he was inspired to write perhaps his best known verses, Ring Out Wild Bells.

The time draws near the birth of Christ;
The moon is hid, the night is still;
A single church below the hill
Is pealing, folded in the mist;

Ring out old shapes of foul disease;
Ring out the narrowing lust of gold;
Ring out the thousand years of old,
Ring in the thousand years of peace.

Ring in the valiant man and free,
The large heart, the kindlier hand;
Ring out the darkness of the land,
Ring in the Christ that is to be.

The Church of The Holy Innocents, High Beech. Here bathed in soft winter sunshine.

Waltham Abbey.

Terling Place, with lovely ornamental gardens. Inset the nearby church of St. Mary, Roman red tile can be seen in the walls.

One only has to turn off the main roads which cross Essex to be in countryside of gentle lanes and villages of age-old charms. Terling, just a few miles from the busy A12 is set in the heart of unspoilt countryside. The village has a fine working 'smock mill' gleaming white so that when flying above the Essex countryside it beckons towards the village. Terling has one of the finest modern houses in Essex, Terling Place, a house with magnificent gardens best viewed from the privileged position about 1000 feet above. There are a scattering of farms and buildings of the Tudor Age and many must have been known by Henry VIII, for he had a palace in Terling.

Nearby Fairstead could hardly be more remote. The name comes from the Saxon meaning a fair and pleasant place, and so it is! It is approached by a winding lane from Terling, the church with a spire dating from the reign of Queen Elizabeth I is set on a much earlier tower and surrounded with sycamores, limes and chestnuts. Essex has little stone but an abundance of flint and pebble and there must have been a nearby 'quarry', perhaps a Roman Villa. So the builders of St. Mary's at Fairstead about 700 years ago built the church with flint and pebble and where a good shape was required, round the windows, doors and corners of the walls, the local materials were reinforced with typical Roman tile taken from a nearby Roman building.

During a restoration in 1890, plaster was stripped from the walls to reveal 13th century wall paintings, truly the church of St. Mary Fairstead is a medieval art gallery.

Stansted Airport and the vast new terminal.

Not too far from Cressing Temple is another huge building, this time the architecture is modern. It is the new terminal at Stansted Airport. The runway is nearly two miles long and on a good day when climbing out from Southend, the vast 'gash' is clearly visible, dominated by the new terminal at the south eastern corner.

Essex Showground and Leighs Priory

When flying above the countryside, often a piece of 'dead' straight road comes into view, such a straight road is sure to have its origins in the Roman period. From our county town of Chelmsford, a straight road reaches north east towards Braintree. By the side of this road is the Essex Show Ground, a bustle of country activities for a few days in midsummer. Yet just a mile or two away is one of the most secluded and delightful places in all Essex, Leighs Priory *(Leez is its ancient spelling)* again looking best from above especially in a soft evening sunshine. Founded in 1220 for the Augustinian Canons it is set in the wooded valley of the river Ter. Where the gracious red brick buildings, topped with Elizabethan chimneys together with ruins of the monastery produce a harmony hardly equalled anywhere. This place, once the home of hooded monks, of great lords and ladies, was occupied by the royalists during the civil war from whence, on the approach of the parliamentary troops they retreated to Colchester. The terrible Siege of Colchester, where Royalists suffered much, was the last major event of that war.

Leez has a long, colourful and fascinating history and one wonders if the present owners see the ghosts of the previous residents as they walk the gentle paths in the shade of the great gatehouse.

Essex Showground.

Leighs Priory, Great Leighs.

Layer Marney Towers, touched by a late afternoon sun.

Tomb of Lord Henry Marney. Died 24th May, 1523.

Another great gatehouse at Layer Marney has dominated the surrounding countryside for some 400 years. This splendid Tudor building we see today is just part of a magnificent mansion which was planned by Sir Henry Marney on the site where his family had lived since Norman times. Essex would probably have had the finest house in the country but alas he died and the house was never completed. In 1523 Sir Henry was laid to rest in a splendid tomb of black Cornish marble, in the church he had built beside the house.

The Tranquil Centre

The straightness of the Roman Road is lost in the centre of Braintree now, but it continues straight again on the far side of the town. Another Roman road The Stane Street has its beginning in Colchester *(Roman Camulodunum),* at Marks Tey it makes a junction with a Roman Road from London which can still be seen, this road is now the A12. Stane Street crossed the other road which passed through Braintree in the centre of the town then continued to the west country.

Surprisingly unspoilt is the countryside in the triangular centre of Essex formed by the Stane Street in the north, the A12 to the east with the M11 to the west and a short stretch of the M25 in the south. Just move a mile or two from the turmoil of these main roads and the scene changes to one of gentle lanes and unspoilt villages.

Blackmore

Blackmore is a village of quiet charm with a duck pond, several noteworthy pubs, a church dating from the Norman period and a house known as 'Jericho Priory'. Henry VIII used to visit the monastery in Blackmore, when his courtiers discreetly said, "He is gone to Jericho", a name used to indicate a place of concealment. There his mistress Elizabeth Blount gave birth to a son in 1518 and he was christened Henry Fitzroy, 'son of a king'. Elizabeth was married off to one of Cardinal Wolesey's retainers. The nearby River Can is known as 'the Jordon'.

The village church is called The Priory Church of St. Laurence and there is much of interest both outside and inside, however it is the splendid wooden tower of this fascinating church which is perhaps its finest feature. Medieval joiners cut great oaks from the surrounding forests, laid vast timbers in a square on the ground then, with uprights, crossbeams and braces built the massive tower in three stages securing the joints with oak pegs. The tower has been provided with interior lighting so that a visitor can view this splendid work.

Blackmore Village.

The Priory Church of St. Laurence, Blackmore.

The Priory Church of St. Laurence, detail of 15th century tower construction.

Ongar, the Motte and Bailey Castle can be seen in the foreground.

Not too far from Blackmore is the market town of Chipping Ongar, *(Chipping means market).* Ongar is a delightful town which has a superb Motte and Bailey castle of the Norman period. I expect people walking down the high street and seeing the sign 'castle' expect to see a massive stone keep with an outer wall, the usual image of a castle.

However, the 'castle' is the earliest type of Norman castle, a great mound, a Motte, with an adjacent enclosed area or Bailey, the whole surrounded with a moat, Ongar Castle is still splendid.

Greensted

Just a mile or two from Ongar is the tiny village of Greenstead where set in a sylvan setting is the Saxon church of St. Andrew. This is the oldest wooden church in the world and is thought to date from 845 AD. Now a shrine of universal pilgrimage, it probably owes its survival to its position about two and a half miles east of the Roman road and set deep in the great forest of Waltham which covered much of Essex. The marauding Danes who killed St Osyth and St Edmond in 870 AD would have had great difficulty in finding this remote Saxon church, so we can still enjoy this treasure today.

Greensted, the Saxon Church of St. Andrew nestles in the trees.

The trees which built this church were growing when the Romans came and even now you can run your fingers along the ancient walls and feel the marks made by the Saxon carpenter. Great oaks were felled and split into three; the outer curved sections made the church walls with the curved side out, and the centre plank was used for the roof. In the year 1013 the body of St Edmund rested at Greensted while on its way for re-interment at Bury St Edmunds. There is much more of great beauty and interest at St Andrews. It is well worth a visit for itself and its captivating setting.

Detail of Saxon wooden walls. Painting by Ron Slade.

Doddinghurst

I am fortunate to have my home in the parish of Blackmore, which is vast, but I am rather closer to the village of Doddinghurst, where the 13th century flint faced Church of All Saints also has a superb 14th Century wooden shingled tower. Standing on a site which has had a church from the Saxon times there is evidence of a Norman building in the rear wall of the church and the oak porch is Elizabethan.

This, the longest porch of its kind, is much loved by artists, photographers and courting couples who have enjoyed the shelter and seclusion of the porch since the 16th century. Looking lovely at any time All Saints perhaps looks its most beautiful when covered with winter snow.

The Church of All Saints, Doddinghurst.

The Church of All Saints, Doddinghurst, the Elizabethan timber porch. Painting by Ron Slade.

The Doddinghurst Covenant

The various religious denominations of this 'Domesday Village', Doddinghurst, gathered in the church and in the presence of Derek, Bishop of Bradwell, Thomas, Bishop of Brentwood, The Reverend Brian Galliers and the Reverend John Howden, Rector of All Saints Doddinghurst, a Covenant was presented and signed by all the congregation.

During the celebration of Pentecost Sunday, May 19th 1991

We, therefore, convenant together to make visible the unity of Christ's people in this village and this district.

We pledge ourselves
to pray for each other
to support each other in practical ways in our work, in our witness and in our service within our community
to continue to work for the life and growth of the churches together in this district.

We commit ourselves to the following:
to share in a range of social action in and for our community
to combine, where suitable, our efforts to help the disadvantaged
to share in Christian fellowship, study and prayer
to worship God together in formal and informal acts of worship throughout the year, in full recognition and mutual respect of each others laws and traditions.

We acknowledge and thank God who has called us to make this covenant together.

All Saints Doddinghurst, presenting the Covenant.

Hay Green Lane, Blackmore. Painting by Ron Slade.

Fryerning

Driving from my home I can pass through Hay Green Lane, a very typical Essex Lane, narrow twisting and leafy, seldom is there another car but more often riders, with occasionally a pheasant at the roadside. This lane leads to Fryerning. Near the villages of Fryerning and Mill Green are some surviving tracks of the ancient Forest of Essex . It is here I take my dog Ria to ramble the paths which criss-cross the woods and we so often have this lovely woodland to ourselves although sometimes we meet other ramblers or riders enjoying this remote forest.

It is now Easter, and yesterday, Easter Sunday, Ria and I wandered deep into the woods where far from the road there was a carpet of very delicate wood anemones. Deer still roam the glades, paths and adjacent fields much as they have done since the forests were hunting preserves of kings. The Viper pub, its name recalling some other inhabitants of the woods, is an excellent place to take refreshment after a wander through the ancient woods. Over three centuries old and with its own 'cottage style garden', the Viper is also unique in name in the whole of Britain.

The Church of St. Mary, Fryerning.

Highwood Forest and The Viper Pub

Part of the ancient forest of Highwood and the Viper pub. Inset: Wood Anemones.

The Viper pub. Painting by Ron Slade.

Chelmsford, from the Cathedral looking past the shopping centre and High Street to the Essex County Cricket Ground.

Chelmsford is the County Town of Essex which in 1988 celebrated a hundred years as a borough yet its history extends back past beyond the last ice age for perhaps another forty thousand years. A history which is vividly depicted in a permanent exhibition in the Chelmsford and Essex Museum. In those ancient times when the great forest pressed on both sides of the River Chelmer, stone age man, perhaps when out on a hunting trip, would pause for rest and refreshment by the shallow part of the river, the ford.

Later as the use of metal began to take over from stone the bronze age peoples made their villages around Chelmsford, one has been excavated close to Chelmer Village. They were followed by The Belgic tribe who emigrated here from Flanders around 150 BC and who now used iron. Iron was the great marvel of that time and a settlement of the Belgic Tribe has been discovered on the site now occupied by Marconi Radar, a contemporary wonder. Another Iron Age settlement was found at Little Waltham and an excavation was carried out there in 1971-72 in advance of the construction of the bypass. The Iron Age is considered to end with the coming of the Romans in AD 43 although many of the traditions and much of the Iron Age culture must have remained long into the Roman period.

The Romans called Chelmsford, Caesaromagus, which means Ceasar's Market, and so it became, now much of the Roman town is buried beneath the area centred on Moulsham Street. As buildings in the area are demolished for rebuilding, excavations occur and our knowledge of Caesaromagus grows.

The Roman period gave way to the Saxon as the tribes moved into the lush forests and country of Essex from Northern Europe. With their arrival went much of the culture of the Roman way of life, the buildings fell into decay, the well-built bridges collapsed and the river crossing again becoming a ford.

The owner of the land through which the river flowed was named Coelmer, so the ford where travellers crossed was called Coelmer's Ford, which later became Chelmsford and after some years the river became the Chelmer.

By the time of William the Conqueror the important Roman town was forgotten, and Chelmsford was but a hamlet with an annual value entered in the Domesday Book of only eight pounds, while neighbouring Moulsham had a value of twelve pounds.

In the twelfth century, the Lord of the Manor, The Bishop of London, recognised the strategic position of Chelmsford and again bridged the Rivers Can and Chelmer. These bridges with the old Roman road which linked London with the North East (now the A12) together with the granting of a charter to hold a weekly market, and later a licence for an annual fair, ensured the growth and prosperity of the town into Chelmsford, the Cathedral City we know today.

In the centre of the town is the Shire Hall, a splendid building dating from 1790. The graceful front has four pillars crowned with a pediment on which are figures representing Justice, Wisdom and Mercy.

It seems ironic that with those statues adorning it that the Shire Hall stands on the site of an older court, an assize, notorious for the infamous witch trials that took place there some three hundred years ago. On one day in 1645, nine poor women were sent to the stake.

The Cathedral of St. Mary, only raised to cathedral rank in 1913, has been standing in its churchyard , now a lovely peaceful 'green oasis' in the centre of the city, for about 500 years. With graceful 15th century spire and a splendid richly panelled two storey porch. In the middle ages before the time of Shakespeare, Chelmsford was famous for its religious plays, perhaps through a connection with the 'Black Friars' who had built a Friary at the end of Moulsham Street. This tradition continued until protestant times with the players from Chelmsford loading their wagons and taking their plays around the county. Sadly no script has survived but the tradition lives on; in May each year, centred on the Cathedral, is presented a feast of music, poetry and drama, 'The Chelmsford Festival'.

Moulsham, this urban sprawl covers what is left of the Roman Town, Caesaromagus.

Chelmsford Cathedral and Shire Hall.

Mountnessing Windmill, a post mill built in 1807. This mill can be seen working on open days, and you can even buy the flour produced.

Ingatestone Hall, probably the finest Tudor courtyard house in the country. It is open to the public.

Brentwood looking across the High Street to the Anglican Cathedral of St. Thomas, The Roman Catholic Cathedral of St. Mary and St. Helen's to Brentwood School next to which can be seen the William Hunter Memorial. To the right is part of the Ursuline Convent School.

Brentwood is long famous as a coaching stage on the old Roman road from London and is rightly proud of its public school founded by Sir Anthony Browne in 1557 and the date 1558 can easily be seen over the door of one of the early buildings. From Brentwood School a young man left to join the R.A.F. and he wrote a letter to his mother before setting out on his first raid.

He did not return from the raid, but afterwards the letter was first published in The Times and later by many other papers of the English speaking world. Everybody who read the letter was deeply moved and inspired at the time of Dunkirk.

Another young man of Brentwood was William Hunter, an apprentice who would not recant the scriptures and was burned to death by an elm tree in front of Brentwood School. As he was dying William cried out "Son Of God Shine Upon Me", and immediately the scene was lighted by the sun.

We have in Essex two of the oldest places of worship in Britain, St. Peter's-On-The-Wall and Greensted, now opposite the school we have one of the newest. There has been built a new Roman Catholic Cathedral which was dedicated to St. Mary and St. Helen on the 30th May 1991.

Brentwood School.

The Cathedral of St. Mary and St. Helen, Brentwood.

Weald Country Park

Weald Country Park is situated adjacent to South Weald village just to the west of Brentwood, and is one of seven country parks owned and adminstered on behalf of us all by Essex County Council.

Weald Country Park. Inset: Illustration of medieval Ha-Ha.

For at least 700 years there has been a park at South Weald, yet there is evidence in the form of the remnants of an Iron Age Hill Fort in the park which proves that the area was used between 500 B.C. and 50 A.D. by 'Ancient Britons'. Like many medieval parks it was used for hunting deer which were abundant, with some truly wild deer still roaming the park until the 1950's.

Some deer have been returned to the park within a compound, and now, (1992), there is talk of a vast new area being contained where visitors will once again be able to walk amongst the deer. This compound will have a tall fence, but in medieval trimes to prevent deer wandering they constructed a 'Ha-Ha', a ditch with a shallow gradient one side and steep one the other so the deer could not cross, a very effective measure which cleverly did not spoil the landscape. In the 18th and 19th centuries the medieval hunting park gave way to a landscaped park much as we see today. We now have over 400 acres of woods, meadows, lakes and ponds, one notable feature is the 'Chestnut Avenue' which is most beautiful when the trees wear their autumn colours.

However, we can enjoy the park and its abundance of wildlife in all the seasons, the winter, with the trees covered with snow and the wildfowl walking on the frozen lake is an especially lovely time.

Weald Country Park—The lake in winter.

Basildon and Rayleigh

Basildon and Eastgate Shopping Centre.

So, from just south of Brentwood, still very much rural Essex, the very busy A127 leads back to Southend past Basildon with Towngate, the new theatre, and a number of retail parks adjacent to the main road to the south, and Rayleigh to the north.

Basildon for the most part is a new town and Rayleigh, a stronghold on the hills, is ancient, and for centuries it has dominated the high ground between the valleys of the River Thames and River Crouch. Mentioned in the Domesday Book, the town has a magnificent example of a Norman Motte and Bailey castle, a type in which Essex abounds, although at Rayleigh the typical shape of mound and enclosure with a ditch and moat all round it, are difficult to define, for it is much overgrown.

The original Motte and Bailey castle was built by Swein and it is this earthwork, rising 50 feet above the town we can enjoy today, of the later stone keep and walls not a stone remains. However, in the nearby church are still vestiges of construction from Swein's day. There is Norman work in the chancel walls and a font where the Normans dedicated their little ones to Christ. The tower has dominated the church for some 500 years and the bell which still rings may have told the Rayleigh people of the victory at Agincourt. There must have been a Roman building nearby for there are Roman red tiles strengthening the walls, now nearby stands a windmill. Built in 1798, this tower mill with a distinctive white cap, which turns the sails into wind, beckons travellers to Rayleigh for miles around and from every direction. The ground floor of the mill houses the museum which has exhibits donated by local people and depicting life in Rayleigh in bygone times.

The road to Benfleet must have been a narrow lane then, as it meandered past the old pub 'The Paul Pry', Rayleigh Weir, and so to Thundersley, Hadleigh and Benfleet. In recent times where the old road crossed the new A127 there became a notorious bottleneck. This at last has been relieved with the construction of an underpass.

Rayleigh, The Mount and Windmill. The Mount is another example of a Norman Motte and Bailey Castle.

The Paul Pry, on the Rayleigh Road, as it was in 1865. Inset: As it is in 1992. Photograph courtesy of Shirley Stead, Thundersley.

The Rayleigh Weir underpass, almost finished but open. Inset: The roundabout at the commencement of work.

Southend

Southend was at one time the playground of the East End, I can remember in my young days hundreds of coaches setting out from London for the day at the seaside. Although the town still has much of a resort atmosphere, industrial activity now dominates.

Southend, the High Street.

Southend Pier, the paddle steamer Waverley is trying to berth in a heavy sea.

Peter Pan's Playground.

The Royal Terrace.

A young lady from the East End of London wrote in her school book .....

A Visit To The Seaside

During the summer monthe many people visit the seaside.
Last year I went to visit my cousins in Leigh.
We used to go down to the water every morning and stay till dinner time.
Sometimes we used to go in the train to Rayleigh and spend the afternoon at my grandfathers.
Rayleigh is a very pretty place, but there are only a few houses.
Sometimes we would walk a mile and see only one house.
If the children that live outside the village wanted to go to school they would have to walk about three miles.
Another pretty walk is as far as Prittle-well.
We walked from Prittle-well to Leigh one afternoon and only met one person on the road until we reached Leigh.
If it was too hot we used to sit on the hills in front of the sea and watch the men act who went by the name of 'The Jollity Boys'.
One afternoon my cousins and I went for a walk to Hadleigh and saw the remains of Hadleigh Castle.

By Elsie Bates aged 11, 7th July, 1905.

Our thanks to Shirley Stead for the use of this letter. Elsie Bates was Shirley's great great aunt.

A flight from the west along the river brings the aircraft over the Norman remains of Hadleigh Castle, the surrounding area now a country park, across Old Leigh with its cockle sheds, past the pier which has defied several disasters over the town and so to a landing on runway '06' at the airport.

Perhaps now you would like to go to one of the local airfields, book an aircraft, and see some of these sights which make Essex *Rich and Beautiful*.

Very often I take the shots while making a gentle turn around the subject, a trick a ground based photographer would find difficult to emulate. So it is that in the short time it takes to fly through one circle I can see a thousand pictures with the changing light, colour, size and shadows producing an immense diversity.

This diversity is probably matched by the people who fly aeroplanes. They come from all walks of life; flying is not just for the rich. It is these differences which make being a flying instructor such a rewarding occupation. Once someone is involved in flying, they are then in a 'club' which is worldwide, with the chance of meeting a fellow flyer in some obscure airport the norm.

Hadleigh Castle in the springtime.

Shellhaven Oil Refinery.

Benfleet Creek and Benfleet Yacht Club.

The Cockle Sheds, Leigh-on-Sea.

Leigh-on-Sea covered in winter snow.

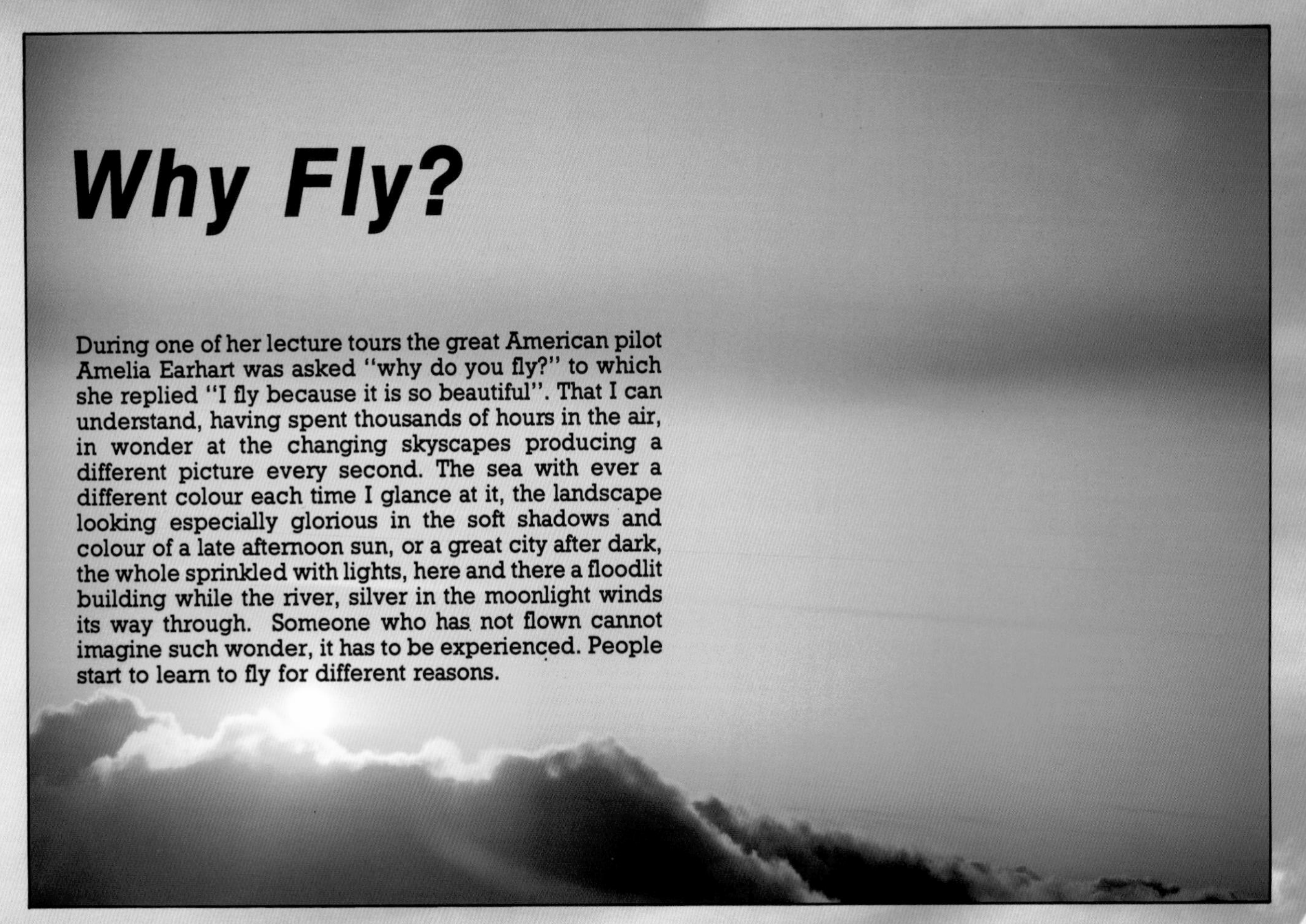

Why Fly?

During one of her lecture tours the great American pilot Amelia Earhart was asked "why do you fly?" to which she replied "I fly because it is so beautiful". That I can understand, having spent thousands of hours in the air, in wonder at the changing skyscapes producing a different picture every second. The sea with ever a different colour each time I glance at it, the landscape looking especially glorious in the soft shadows and colour of a late afternoon sun, or a great city after dark, the whole sprinkled with lights, here and there a floodlit building while the river, silver in the moonlight winds its way through. Someone who has not flown cannot imagine such wonder, it has to be experienced. People start to learn to fly for different reasons.

Lionel North

It was at the Herts and Essex Aero Club at Stapleford Aerodrome that I first met Lionel. At that time I was a flying instructor and Lionel a control engineer with Fords. Lionel was not content to sit back and remain an engineer but perhaps it was the many trips he made abroad in that role which gave him a burning passion to become a pilot, and a commercial pilot. In those days to take a direct path to become a professional pilot was to undertake a full time course, the cost then was about four thousand pounds, even then a lot of money. The other way was to become a flying instructor gain seven hundred hours flying experience, undertake the written exams and so become a commercial pilot. Lionel chose the latter.

When I became Chief Flying Instructor at Southend Light Aviation Centre at Southend Airport, bringing flying training back to Southend after a number of years lapse, Lionel decided to join me. Through 1968 flying most weekends to Calais, Le Touquet and Ostend, Lionel continued to gain experience and increase his flying hours towards the one hundred and fifty he required before he was able to start his flying instructor's course with me. The year moved on and Lionel was unwell on and off, his doctors diagnosed his illness as 'nerves', a less nervous man I have not known.

The new year came, he still had thirty hours to complete and so, after a number of weeks thought and planning Lionel set off with a friend (not a pilot) in February 1969 flying Piper Cherokee 'Whiskey Alpha', to fly round the Iberian Peninsular. February is not the best time of the year for such a flight, days are short, with the risk of poor weather high. Lionel flew from Southend to Le touquet, Bordeaux, Oporto, Lisbon and Gibraltar, then to Tangiers and home via Malaga, Alicante, Barcelona, Perpignan. As they flew overhead Toulouse Airport they had a fine view of the then new

Concorde, so on to Le Harve and Southend. The return was a day late due to snow on part of the route. For that trip Lionel received 'The Pilot of The Year' trophy at the flying club's first birthday party.

Lionel North receiving The Pilot of the Year Trophy at Southend Light Aviation Centre from my wife, Cathy.

By now Lionel was more unwell, he attended St. Marks Hospital where his father was told the true nature of the illness; cancer, and was advised not to tell Lionel. His father did come to see me asking if it would be possible for Lionel to complete his instructor course in spite of the fact that he would never be able to instruct.

Pilots need a medical certificate to fly as pilot in command, but during the instructor's course I would be with him all the time and another pilot would be with him during the test. The authorities agreed that I could continue, Colin Beckwith, who is now head of flight crew training agreed to conduct the test. It was difficult for me having to drive Lionel hard, but he was an above average student and passed the course and test with flying colours. The first flying instructor I had trained, and one who was destined not to fly again. I last saw Lionel in St. Mark's Hospital; it was the Thursday evening, the day before the club aircraft were to depart for the Jersey Air Rally. Lionel said "I will probably die tonight".

I asked, "Is there anything I can do for you?"

"Yes," he replied,"will you scatter my ashes over the Thames Estuary from 'Victor Kilo'?

"Of course Lionel."

"What a fabulous last flight", was the response.

As we lined up for take off at Southend for Jersey and the rally, the controller called "Victor Kilo this is the tower."

"Tower, Victor Kilo go ahead."

"Lionel North died in the night", was the message. So it was with a heavy heart that I opened the throttle and took off for the rally.

The funeral was the next week when the club aircraft did a slow fly past at the cemetery led by his beloved 'Victor Kilo'.

A few days later as the sun was setting and the water of the Thames glowed golden in the evening light, alone, I again opened the throttle of 'Victor Kilo', took off, headed south and climbed to one thousand feet off Southend Pier. There I said goodbye to Lionel as he left the aircraft for his 'fabulous last flight'.

Don Delf

It was in the mid sixties that I first met Don Delf. Don was a Southend man but then spent most of his life in Gibraltar. He was master of the 'Mons Calpe' the Gibraltar to Tangiers ferry. The owners were considering changing from ships to hovercraft, and the masters of hovercraft would, as well as their 'masters' ticket' also need a pilot's licence. Don gained his pilot's licence that summer and every summer after that when he was on home leave he would spend a day or two refresher flying while his wife Gladys wiled the time away knitting.

Captain Don Delf, Master of the ferry 'Mons Calpe'.

'Mons Calpe' sails for Gibraltar at dusk.

I last heard of Don when my daughter Elizabeth went to Tangiers on her honeymoon. I said before she went, "try to see Don and find out how he is". Don was still master of the ferry and Elizabeth and Paul had a fabulous crossing, sharing the bridge with the Captain and being served refreshment from the steward. Sadly since that day I have not heard of Don but I am sure one day our paths will cross again, that's the way it is the flying world!

Richard Lowe

About the same time that I met Don, Richard Lowe turned up at the Herts and Essex Aero Club to learn to fly. Richard, a director of Rank films, decided to fly for quite a different reason, he was scared of flying! Although he had been an army tank commander, the thought of flying was frightening, a not uncommon fear. So it was that Richard showing a courage which was characteristic of the man decided that the way to conquer the fear was to learn to fly. Some flying instructors feel the need to 'show off' and Richard unfortunately had one of these for his very first flight. They took off on the downhill runway; as the aircraft gained a little height the instructor saw a car passing along the road at the end of the runway. "We'll scare the life out of him", he shouted, pushing the control column of the Aircoupe forward to dive straight at the car, pulling the aircraft up at the last minute into a steep climb. Richard made the instructor land. Although of course unhappy, Richard having made up his mind, was not deterred and next time he came for a lesson I became his instructor. Richard gained his licence, subsequently became an instructor and we have been friends ever since.

The Cathedral Square, Pisa, Tuscany, Italy.

During the time Richard was gaining both his hours and experience we shared a couple of memorable flights. The first, to Naples where Richard had a business conference, another Richard joined the flight, Dick Cole (of R. G. Cole, Grays).

The day 'Papa Victor' a Cherokee 180 rolled down the runway for take off was bright and clear, our flight took us across Kent past Dover into France at Calais, flying north of Paris and so into the Rhone Valley at Dijon then south for a landing at Lyon to refuel. I have long had an interest in the Roman world and our flight south was to take us past many famous places of the Roman period. The day was superb as we circled a number of ancient theatres, amphitheatres and the great aqueduct, The Pont du Gard, then continuing south to Montelimar and climbing to twelve thousand feet before turning east to cross the Maritime Alps.

Soon St. Tropez and the brilliant Mediterranean came into view and we could start our let down, back to three thousand feet, to follow the coast. Past Nice and Monte Carlo and the Italian border at Ventimiglia and soon after passing Genova we turned south again flying a few miles out from the coast. Pisa looked magnificent with the 'Leaning Tower' looking bizarre in the magnificent

Roman Theatre, Arles, France.

cathedral square. There, with permission from air traffic control we did a couple of turns, and took some shots of the famous Tower the Cathedral and Baptistry. This is the sort of thing it is possible to do in a light aircraft, but not in a 'Boeing 747'. The sun was getting quite low as we passed Rome and setting behind the Isle of Ischia as we turned over the Bay of Naples for the airport, where we landed at dusk.

We were three quite big men and the only car available was a Fiat 500 Topolino. Once Richard's conference was complete we spent a few days exploring what is now amongst my favourite places, Naples, Sorrento and the Salurno Peninsular.

Richard Lowe at Faro Airport, Portugal.

The little car with Richard of necessity doing a 'tank commander act' was head and shoulders through the sunroof! I felt sorry for one signoria who, while we were driving in the middle of Naples was so intrigued by the sight she ran her Ferrari into the rear of another car. 'Topolino' took us to the summit of Vesuvius, to Pompeii and round what Goethe called 'The Golden Coast', the Salerno Peninsular, where we stopped at Sorento under an orange tree for refreshment. Richard, who had travelled much in the United States and northern Europe was quite intrigued to be sipping his drink beneath a tree with 'real oranges' growing. Now when I visit Sorrento I look at that orange tree and I am reminded of that fabulous flight and Richard.

The time came to return but before setting course north we flew over Pompeii and the Greek temples at Paestum.

Afterwards when we gave an illustrated talk to the other club members Richard remarked, "Edward does not measure his distances in miles like other pilots, he uses Roman Theatres".

Keith Foster

It was a Sunday, March 3rd, 1968 when I brought flying training back to Southend Airport with one Piper Cherokee and an Aircoupe, and as I opened the doors one of the first persons I met was Keith Foster the postman. Keith's 'walk' included the airport but that was not chance, Keith's passion, ever since he could remember, was flying and everything connected with it.

So Keith arranged to include Southend Airport in his duties, to be near aircraft, but becoming a pilot seemed an impossible dream. The easiest part of running a flying school is getting the flying staff; that's the glamorous part; however there are thousands of other chores, often quite tedious, which have to be done. That Sunday Keith offered to help me about the club during his time off duty as a postman. The unstinting help he gave was invaluable, preparing the room for evening lectures, cleaning, redecorating and so on. In fact he became my 'Man Friday'. Keith did achieve his ambition during this time, he gained his Private Pilot's Licence. It was a very sad day for me when Keith left the club and an even sadder day when he died a year or two later.

Wendy Crick

"I dare you to take a trial flying lesson", remarked a friend to Wendy as they looked at the advertisement in the local paper. Wendy was unable to resist the challenge and that was the start of her love of, and career in flying.

That trial lesson developed into a Private Pilot's Licence but Wendy was not content to stop there and while she continued her flying her talent came through and she received the club's Pilot of the Year trophy which now in honour of Lionel was renamed 'The Lionel North Trophy'. Soon she had enough hours and she completed an instructor course with me. After which she instructed at Southend until she was able to gain her Commercial Pilots Licence.

Now Wendy could fly airliners! She joined British Air Ferries and became a first officer on the Carvairs, until they were phased out and she went back to instructing, perhaps the most rewarding task in flying. Wendy became the first woman to teach would-be commercial pilots at the British Airways school of flying at Hamble in Hampshire. Eventually Hamble was closed and after several different flying jobs she became an examiner with the Civil Aviation Authority, first examining commercial pilots and now in flight operations.

First Officer Wendy Crick is at the controls of this British Air Ferries Carvair as, loaded with cars and passengers it heads for Ostend. Inset: Wendy with the Lionel North Trophy.

Dick Cole

Dick and I were old friends, having spent many hours diving under sea, exploring and filming, the film we helped make about the little known Devonshire cup coral (caryophyllia smithii) won a gold and two bronze medals at the underwater film festival in Santa Monica, but that is another story. In 1966 Dick and his wife joined Cathy, my wife, and myself, and we flew in a Piper Tripacer to the Jersey Air Rally. The flight was wonderful and the hospitality we received from the Channel Islands Aero Club for that fabulous weekend was 'out of this world'. The Jersey Air Rally is probably the most prestigious in Europe with the major awards hotly contended by about one hundred and fifty entries from about ten countries. Prizes are given for flight preparation, flight plan, navigation, concours, air law, aircraft recognition with the 'Piccadilly Trophy' (The Grand Prix) going to the best overall. That year the great lady pilot Sheila Scott won the Grand Prix.

At the banquet after the award presentations, Dick, who had never been in a light aircraft until coming to Jersey announced, "I am going to win the 'Piccadilly Trophy", I was taken aback!

Dick Cole (left) at the Jersey Air Rally receiving the 'Piccadilly Trophy' 1970.

Dick Cole and Vera Greagg at the Jersey Air Rally, 1971.

During a pilot's flying training he is required to fly at least ten hours solo which must include some cross country flying. Dick took off solo from Stapleford one nice summer day for a triangular navigation exercise. He became a little lost during the detail and seeing a disused airfield below, landed. One thing I vividly remember about Dick was his great broad smile and I can imagine that huge grin as he taxied up beside some workmen brewing tea over a brazier. "Where am I?", asked our pilot, "This is Castle Camps, mate! Want a cup of tea?", they replied. After the vast mug of tea, Dick asked the way to Stapleford, "that way", came the reply as they pointed in a general southerly direction. With a 'wiggle' of his wings after getting airborne, Dick turned in the direction indicated and found Stapleford. However, the broad smile faded when Eric Thurston, the Chief Flying Instructor at the time debriefed on the affair. It was a special day for Dick when the first step towards winning the 'Piccadilly Trophy' at Jersey was achieved, the Private Pilot's Licence. Hard work and continuation training followed and eventually ready in 1970, he entered the Jersey Air Rally.

Dick achieved his dream, which was his reason for learning to fly. He was proud to receive the 'Piccadilly Trophy' together with the 'Lannoy Cup' (highest points for general navigation) a far cry from Castle Camps, The Aircraft Recognition Prize, the 'Krichefski Trophy', (the best entry from the U.K.) while the aircraft, Cherokee 'Papa Victor' gained the 'Decca Trophy' for 'Concours d'Elegance'.

The following year (1971) Dick entered the rally again this time with several other aircraft from Southend Light Aviation Centre, including Cherokee 'Victor Kilo', piloted by a lady from South Benfleet, Vera Greagg. Dick did well again winning the Lannoy Cup and the Aircraft Recognition Prize again, but in this rally Vera was runner up for the Piccadilly Trophy and won the Isabel Cridland Trophy for best woman pilot, and the Charles Strasser Cup for the best first time entrant. That was quite an achievement by Vera, and there was a bonus, the team won the 'Inter Club Trophy'.

Dick has lived for some years in Eire where he is now president of the Waterford Flying Club. Remembering his first ambition in flying he still attends the Jersey Air Rally most years.

With a Piper Tripacer at Stapleford Airfield, about to depart for Jersey, 1966. Dick and Joan Cole, myself and my wife Cathy.

Vera Greagg

Vera's love of flying began in the early thirties when, blond hair streaming in the wind she flew in an open cockpit biplane from the small grass airfield at Prittlewell. The flight was with 'Sir Alan Cobhams Flying Circus'. Vera might even hve been flown by that great pioneer pilot who, a little later, in the thirties, opened up the long distance air routes, especially from London to South Africa. Those routes were soon to be followed by the wonderful aircraft of the period especially the beautiful 'C' class flying boats, which design was later to be developed into the Sunderland.

In those far off days, the early thirties, unlike now, not too many people considered it possible to learn to fly. However the thrill and exhilaration of that first flight has remained with Vera to this day. It was to be nearly forty years later that Vera came to the flying club, flew in a light aircraft once more and the 'bug' took hold. Vera gained her Private Pilot's Licence and as you have read was successful in the Jersey Air Rallly. For a while she ran an air charter company on Southend Airport often flying in 'twins' to various destinations in Europe. Sadly, as with us all, things change and she has not flown in command of an aircraft for some years. Vera says now, "the ten years I was flying were the happiest of my life".

Vera Greagg and Cherokee 'Victor Kilo' in Jersey, 1971.

Roy Mann

Flying was in Roy's family blood. His father had been a wartime pilot, and after the war went into commercial aviation. First with B.O.A.C. flying Avro York; a civilian derivation of the Lancaster Bomber. Followed by various aircraft including the DC3, Rapide, Viscount and Comet and had been flying airliners for about twenty years by the time Roy was old enough to fly. Roy had a lot of natural ability quickly gaining his Private Pilot's Licence, a first step. Then, to keep costs down, he flew a single seat 'Turbulent' powered with a Volkswagon engine for many hours above the fields of Essex, I expect he knows those fields better than myself. It was a great pleasure flying with Roy during his instructor's course, and after successfully passing his instructor test, Roy worked with me as a flying instructor for the next two years. During that time many gained from Roy's skill and good humoured instruction.

With his commercial licence achieved, he went to British Midland, my last memory of Roy flying at Southend is of Roy, captain on the last flight of a DC3 operated by British Midland. During that flight Roy decided to give all of us on the ground a treat. After control clearance the DC3 approached from the north, made a slow pass over the runway, went around then swooped in for a fast last pass, before climbing away and disappearing to the south; goodbye DC3, and I did not hear from Roy again until a few days ago, (it is now March 1992).

I walked into Seawing Flying Club on Southend Airport and a voice greeted me from the tea bar, 'hi Edward! Remember me?", although about twenty years had passed I replied "yes, you're Roy Mann". We of course reminisced on the past and talked of the present. Roy is now Boeing 747 fleet captain with Cathay Pacific and lives in Hong Kong.

Captain Roy Mann with Boeing 747 at Singapore.

Rita Boniface

During the war I served with the Royal Air Force in Persia and Iraq and there met Jim Dunbar. Soon after starting flying at Southend in 1968 the NatWest bank posted Jim to London. He bought a house at Thorpe Bay and we renewed our friendship. Rita, a colleague at Jim's bank heard him speak of the 'crop-marks' I was studying in Essex, she was also interested in archaeology. It was midsummer, the marks were prolific, so it was arranged that Rita and a friend would fly with me over Essex exploring the past. That flight was fantastic and Rita enjoyed it so much she decided to learn to fly.

There is a lot to learn, and Rita found it all difficult, but the day came when Rita was ready for her solo cross country.

I authorised the flight and away she went. It was a nice day and I was outside the club pondering a chief flying instructor's role when Laurie, Rita's husband turned up, "where is Rita?" he asked, "she is on a cross country flight", I replied, Laurie turned pale, "don't worry, I told him, "the aircraft will join the circuit over there (pointing) in seven minutes". So it did. After landing, and shutting down the aircraft Rita came up to us and said, "Laurie I have been lost, I was so glad when the airfield came into view", as it happened, exactly on time.

During her further training, Rita won the 'Hogg Robinson Gardner Mountain Award' for instrument flying (flying blind), and was presented with the award by Prince Charles on behalf of the British Woman Pilot's Association.

To Rita flying did not come easy, she really had to work at it and especially the flying instructor's rating which she also achieved. Students subsequently loved to fly with her and I am sure that was because she had found flying difficult and so, had a lot of sympathy and understanding with those would be pilots who were not 'naturals'.

Rita Boniface receiving her award from H.R.H. Prince Charles.

Chris Burke

Chris however, was a 'natural', but when I first met him that would not have been my opinion. It was in 1969, in the days when boys wore their hair shoulder length, Chris was 15 and his hair style was in fashion, it puzzles me now as to why that influenced my opinion, perhaps it was my service training! "Since Chris could first express a desire he has been determined to fly airliners", said his mum, Margaret. I outlined a flying programme, and told them of the requirements and likely cost, not expecting anything to come of it.

One can start to learn to fly at any age but as we have learned there is a requirement for ten hours solo flying in the private pilot's course (every pilot's first step) and seventeen is the youngest age one can fly an aircraft solo. Chris soon started his training and very quickly demonstrated a lot of natural aptitude. His seventeenth birthday dawned bright, with a gentle breeze, a perfect day for flying. After a couple of take offs and landings with myself Chris was ready for his first solo. He flew 'Whiskey Alpha', a piper Cherokee once round Southend Airport on that birthday. A 'first solo' is every pilot's never to be forgotten or repeated experience.

Training progressed with more periods of flying with an instructor and longer solo practices until the course is completed with flying tests and written exams. While Chris gained the needed experience he won the Club's 'Lionel North Trophy', eventually becoming an instructor. After instructing for a couple of years he gained his commercial pilot's licence and left the Southend area. When I last heard of Chris he was Chief Pilot with Manx Airways in the Isle of Mann.

Chris Burke.

Norman Turner

Norman was introduced to light aircraft flying because his sister and brother in law had their own aircraft a 'Rallye' Golf Golf (its call sign) in which he had made a number of flights and became 'hooked' on flying. He flew many hours in that aircraft and in the Piper Cherokee 'Xray Kilo' which replaced it, just for the joy of flying. Norman has made numerous trips, especially to the Mediterranean coast and islands like Elba. But my most vivid memory of Norman was returning to Southend from a flight in the north of England. Before he entered Southend Airport's Special Rules Zone, he had a radio failure. No big problem. He landed, non-radio at Andrewsfield, a perfectly safe procedure.

It was the Saturday before Christmas when Norman and I took off in a Cherokee from Southend for Andrewsfield to rescue 'Golf Golf'. Taxiing in at Andrewsfield we passed 'Golf Golf' and I parked the Cherokee beyond the clubhouse.

Once in the aircraft for departure we would have no communication so I briefed Norman. "When you see me taxi past, tuck in close behind and follow me to the runway. After take off still stay close and do everything I do". I went to control to pay the fees and tell the Duty pilot of our intentions; a 'kids' party was in full swing in the clubhouse. In the meantime Norman had gone to the Rallye to complete the pre-flight checks and start the engine in preparation for our departure. Formalities complete, I left the clubhouse and saw a Cherokee taxi by, I took no notice until, as the Cherokee passed Norman, he tucked in behind. At that time Andrewsfield was non radio, there was no way of getting in touch.

The Cherokee lined up on the runway, rolled for takeoff and there following my instructions but the wrong aircraft, was 'Golf Golf' tucked in close behind. Out came the 'kids' to watch. Now airborne the aircraft turned right round the airfield, Norman followed! The turns continued until the two were lined up with the runway, then, to cheers from the children the Cherokee

Norman Turner (inset) and Rally 'Golf Golf' flying over North Essex.

did a fast pass over the runway! There was Norman close behind. The Cherokee turned right again, I can imagine that Norman, still following was becoming rather irate. Round the airfield once more, this time for a slow flypast to continuing cheers and waves from the children and onlookers. Once more round the circuit, this time the Cherokee came in to land with Norman still close behind. The aircraft taxied in and when the engines were shut down the children with their attendants moved forward. Norman, stern faced now leapt from Golf Golf, went towards the Cherokee when its door opened. Norman was very surprised not to see me, for, with a "Yo Ho Ho" out of the Cherokee, with a massive sack and a long white beard stepped Father Christmas!

Master Philip Avery, aged 8

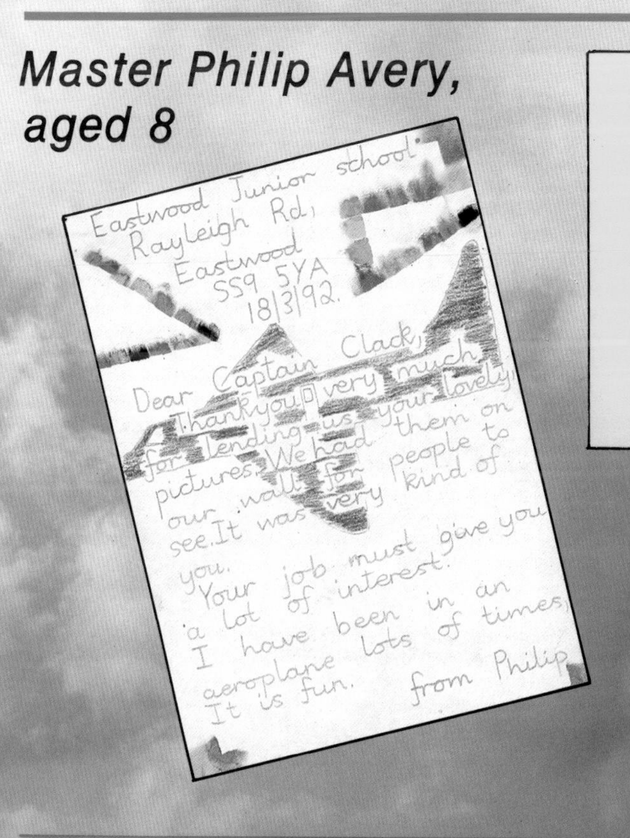

Eastwood Junior school
Rayleigh Rd,
Eastwood
SS9 5YA
18/3/92.

Dear Captain Clack,
Thank you very much for lending us your lovely pictures. We had them on our wall for people to see. It was very kind of you.
Your job must give you a lot of interest.
I have been in an aeroplane lots of times.
It is fun. from Philip

Teacher Kitty Theobald of Eastwood Junior School saw my exhibition of aerial photography and aerial archaeology in Southend Museum. When it had finished she borrowed some of the pictures for use in her class as the subjects fitted nicely into the schools curriculum. When Kitty returned the prints there was a letter from each of her eight year old charges. The letters are a delight. Philip's is reproduced here, the way this young man has used the silhouette of the aircraft with the words is most artistic.
Perhaps in the future Philip when asked, "why do you fly?" will reply, "because of the aerial photographs I saw at school way back in 1992, and in any case, It's fun".

Nothing stands still, pilots move on in their careers, private pilots continue to take friends to lunch in Le Touquet, that is, until the changes wrought by the passage of time force a change. So it is with the aircraft we fly, like the people who fly them the years bring changes to design, the many flying hours make them weary and eventually the time comes when their useful life is at an end.

I am sure every flyer has a twinge of heartache when they see a great aircraft at the end of its life, even if it is one they have not been privileged to fly, like the giant Blackburn Beverley.

The End Of A Giant

My day started much as usual, I met my student flying instructor at Southend Airport where I soon began the role of pretending to be a student pilot, for I teach other pilots how to instruct in flying. My trainee instructor has to give me a 'briefing' on the ground on the lesson to be instructed in the air then with me in the left seat, the seat normally occupied by the captain of the aircraft, teach me that detail. We spent an hour in the classroom while I had a briefing on stalling, which was to be the air exercise. During the briefing I made comments and suggestions as necessary, then it was time to fly, the day was lovely and clear, the aircraft was checked out, and we were ready to go. When I am teaching a pilot how to instruct I have to act the part of a student pilot, in the aircraft I occupy the left seat, the seat normally used by the pilot in charge. My student instructor will, while acting the roll of flying instructor, 'teach me to fly' from the right hand side. After all the years I have been playing this role I know most of the 'stunts' a student pilot can pull and as a consequence I am not a 'very good student' and I expect my 'instructor' to correct my mistakes. Having said that I must not get complacent or my next real trainee will be sure to do something I have not encountered before.

Since this detail was to be stalling I could relax until the aircraft became clear of the airfield and at an altitude of 4500 feet. The approach to the runway was clear, we received our departure clearance and lined up on the runway for take-off. My student, Daryl, smoothly opened the power the engine presures and temperatures were good (the instrument needles over their green arcs) and the engine was developing full power, with the brakes released the aircraft accelerated when the airspeed indicated 55 mph, Daryl eased the control column back and the Cessna became airborne. As we climed out I glanced down to the area which was once 'The Historic Aircraft Museum'. The museum had been closed some years ago and all the aircraft were sold and moved except for the lonely Blackburn Beverley. This aircraft was so vast that the problems involved in moving it were too great to be undertaken. So it remained, alone on the plot where it had once been surrounded by other veteran aircraft. As I looked down I was surprised to see a number of vehicles and machines around the Beverley; the engines were scattered, the immense wings were truncated; this magnificent aircraft was being broken for scrap!

My thoughts flashed back to the day, how long ago was it? 5-10 years, when I flew from Southend to rendezvous with the Beverley over Brentwood in Essex? That day started with a call from our local newspaper, 'The Evening Echo' "can you get airborne and take some shots of a Blackburn Beverley making its last flight from Boscombe Down to Southend?" I was asked, I was of course delighted and was quickly on my way to the airport.

There were arrangements to make, for it is not permitted to format with another aircraft without liaison between the two commanders, so I made a phone call to R.A.F. Boscome Down. In a conversation with the Beverley pilot, Sqd.Ldr Watts-Phillips, we arranged to rendezvous over Brentwood, where I, in my little Piper Cherokee, would escort the Beverley to Southend Airport. We met over Brentwood as arranged, then for the next 15 minutes I enjoyed a most thrilling flight and a magnificent sight as I flew in formation with the great aircraft just a few yards to my left. During the flight I took a number of photographs until we were on the approach to the runway. There, I broke away and Sqd.Ldr Watts-Phillips made a low fly past over the airfield to the delight of the hundreds of people who had turned up to witness the end of that historic flight.

I landed back at Southend from my training flight and that evening, on arriving home, I went straight to my scrap-book and turned up the cutting for the 'Last Flight of a Beverley'. It was almost unbelievable, the date was Friday, October 8th, 1971, 18 years ago. Tempus Fugit!

The Beverley remained on the apron at Southend

Blackburn Beverley over Essex approaching Southend.

Blackburn Beverley about to land on runway 24 at Southend Airport.

The Historic Aircraft Museum at Southend—closed, and the Blackburn Beverley a lonely last survivor.

dwarfing the civil airliners alongside it, while preparations were made for the aircraft to be moved across the airfield to the museum. Fences were removed, power and telegraph lines taken down and the ground prepared before this mighty aircraft could be towed to its new home at the Museum. Now, even if it were possible to restore the Beverley to flying condition the route to the runway is no longer available as so much development has since taken place between the museum site and the air active side of the airfield.

Soon after its arrival at the museum the curator organised a cocktail party within the massive Beverley, and I had the good fortune to be invited. A bar was set up within the capacious hull and about 50 guests enjoyed that memorable evening. The fuselage was clear of any obstruction except for a ladder against one side which lead up to the flight deck, navigator and radio operators positons. In those days the nerve centre of this giant was still pristine and although the aircraft was stationary it was quite thrilling to sit in the captain's position and to imagine flying it, which was easy, for the ground was more than 30 feet below.

The Beverley was designed to fulfil the R.A.F.'s need for a long range universal freighter especially in the troop carrying and paratroop role. For the latter use, two great clam like doors could be opened at the rear of the main fuselage, above these doors the rest of the fuselage was very slender where it extended back to the tail. This arrangement gave a very clear exit for the paratroops and supplies.

The Beverley had an empty weight of about 35 tons and an AUW (all up weight) of about 60 tons. It was powered with four Bristol centaurus engines of 2850 hp each, yet in spite of all that power, performance was lacking.

The actual aircraft at Southend first flew on July 5th, 1958 and was the only example to fly the Atlantic.

However, this aircraft was not destined to fly with the R.A.F., it spent its entire operational life with the Aeroplane and Armament Experimental Establishment at Boscombe Down, during which time it was often seen at low level over Salisbury Plain testing new dropping techniques.

A number of Beverleys were based in Borneo and Sarawak during 1963-65 where they operated with great success dropping supplies and paratroops into the jungle clearings where they were a significant factor in helping to end the insurrection.

TMK 304Y

The day after the flight during which I had seen the aircraft being broken I decided to visit the site. It was quite sad to see the once magnificent flying machine being torn apart. However I had the good fortune to meet Mike Patey who was also making a nostalgic visit with the hope of purchasing one or two souvenirs. Mike had been on active service in Borneo during 1963-65 with the Air Dispatch Squadron Royal Corps of Transport and has flown many times in Beverleys dispatching paratroops and supplies into jungle clearings. Now he had come to look once again on the great hull, the vast doors through which he had dispatched so many troops, and the flight deck he at times shared with the flight crew.

We climbed together up the long ladder and into what was once the nerve centre of the aircraft, all round was destruction, most of the instruments, navigation and radio equipment had been ripped out, not by the team now breaking the Beverley, but by vandals who made their unwelcome visits in the years after the end of the museum while the Beverley stood unguarded and alone. We went back a few days later, very little was to be seen of the aircraft. Only a few 'van' sized pieces remained waiting despatch, except that, on the ground, still comparatively intact was the flight deck. It is hoped a home was found for it, perhaps in the museum at Duxford. If so, it will be a lasting memento of the Blackburn Beverley—a Great Giant!

The Beverley was first grounded then sadly broken, someone purchased one engine, and that is being preserved, perhaps the flight deck has also been saved, but that is all. In the past many of mans' achievements have also been destroyed, yet evidence of their existence often exists below the ground. Now, from aircraft flying above, this evidence is often revealed to the flyers in the form of 'crop-marks'.

Ex-dispatcher Mike Patey watches the removal of a propellor.

C

B

A

Hidden Essex

As we go about our day's activities in the towns and villages, or perhaps, when roaming the fields and footpaths, enjoying the splendours of the Essex countryside it is difficult to imagine that much evidence of our forbears exists, invisible most of the time a few inches below the ground. We still have many wonderful buildings in Essex forming a rich heritage from the past. However much of what was created from ancient times through to the present day has disappeared from view, barrows (burial mounds) have been ploughed out, stone and brick buildings 'quarried' for their materials, wooden buildings demolished, ditches filled in. Yet even so those early builders left an indelible signature on our landscape in the form of 'crop-marks'. To those of us who are privileged to fly above the fields, from the spring through the summer until the harvest, strange circles, squares, straight lines, together with other shapes appear in the growing crops, especially corn. From about a thousand feet above, these marks reflect the distinctive shapes of man's past activities, we call them 'crop-marks'.

A complex site near Dedham, here the 'crop-marks' are accentuated by a low sun creating shadows. Double ringed barrow (burial mound) A. Single ringed barrow B. Large enclosure with entrance C. (See text).

What then are 'Crop-marks'?

Fortunately although most of the structures and buildings of the past were easy to destroy the disturbances of the soil which occurred when they were constructed are almost impossible to eradicate. Subtle changes happen in the disturbed soil compared with the surrounding ground.

It is these changes which produce differences in a crop grown above. The crop grows taller, shorter, or a different colour and in the same shapes as the otherwise invisible changes which exist below the surface. It is these revealing signs which can often be seen very clearly from above.

Again near Dedham. The circles are probably barrows within enclosures. Note how the marks spread through several modern fields. (See text).

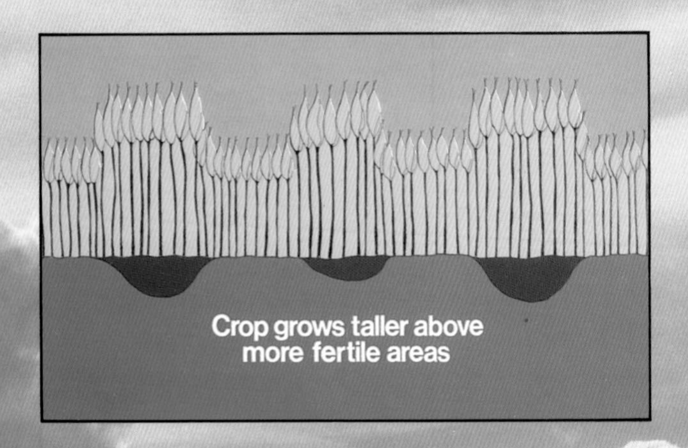

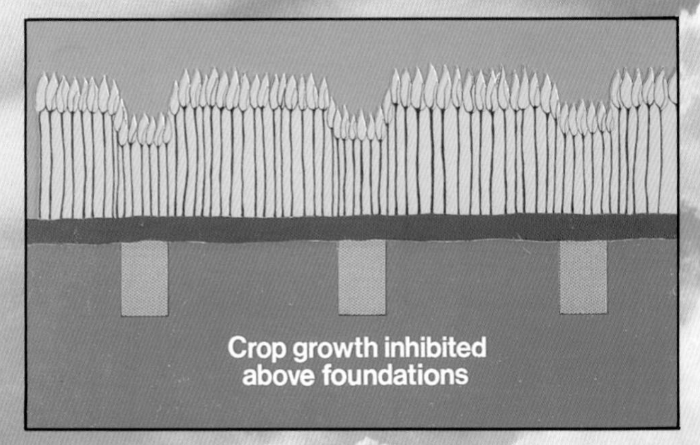

How then are 'crop-marks' formed

Hollows or ditches in the ground later become filled with decaying matter which is often more moist and therefore much more fertile than the adjacent ground. As a consequence a crop above such areas grows taller, with perhaps a different colour and in the same shape (see diagram). Conversely where there are solid foundations just under the surface a crop grown above will be stunted and again the shape will often be clearly defined (see diagram).

Corn crops tend to produce the best 'crop-marks' because of their fast growth. Climate too, has a bearing. A wet spring followed by a dry summer promoting fast ripening with a good differential height seems to be best. It is interesting observing the formation of the marks through the seasons, sometimes they appear early and strongly, to be suppressed by a rainy period, to reappear again when the sun shines. Sometimes the weather stays wet and the yield of 'crop marks' remains poor. Root crops hardly if ever show marks, so that a field with a root crop will be barren of marks, to become a prolific site when, in the same field, the crop is changed to corn.

The best season for observation is from late May through to the harvest. While late afternoon and evening is the best time; when the light from a low soft sun casts long shadows accentuating the marks.

What to look for

Man tends to work in regular shapes, circles, squares, rectangles, straight lines, etc. These shapes then are what we look for, especially when they extend into adjacent fields. The road to Shoeburyness where it passes north of Southchurch is very busy today, much as that area was 3000 years ago about 1200-700 B.C. In a field next to, and only a few yards from the road a massive 'crop-mark' becomes evident most summers. The mark is a vast 'camp' of the Later Bronze Age, *(page 65)* showing as a double symmetrical enclosure (A), entrance clearly showing at (B) together with a round shaped house (C).

Nature's shapes are very beautiful, but for the most part irregular, note a tree or cloud, so that the shapes which we observe in the crops without regular patterns tend to have been created by natural phenomenon. The photograph below has an excellent example of a 'crop-mark' from a man made feature, (The Later Bronze Age Camp) while in the same picture the other marks which cover the field the best I have ever seen of marks created by a natural occurrence. They are 'Ice Wedge Polygons'.

In one of the Ice Ages which extended into Essex, the ground would dry, and a fissure would open up, water would seep into the gap freeze, expand and open the crack more. Later the ice would melt. Then, in time, the opening would fill with more fertile material. Now, when a corn crop is grown on the field the distinctive evidence of the ice age in Essex clearly shows after at least 12,000 years (arrowed).

From ancient times the peoples inhabiting this country have built many great monuments, Stonehenge still dominating the Salisbury Plain being one of the best known. Vast earthworks were constructed, the Wansdyke, built in the 'Dark Ages' still spans about seventy miles of the west country. A similar distance is covered in Northumberland by Hadrian's Wall; with its many turrets, storage depots and forts still visible above ground. One, Housesteads *(see picture page 22)* being a magnificent and typical Roman fort. Much of what remains in Northumberland is due to the inhospitable nature of the country which left many of the ancient structures largely undisturbed by man.

Essex with its gentle favourable climate had most of the materials of early structures re-used in later buildings. So that little remains of our ancient past above ground. There are some superb timber framed buildings dating from medieval times, and in which Essex is very rich. Of these 'Cressing Temple' (see picture page 29) with two great barns probably the most magnificent example. 'Cressing Temple' was the earliest English settlement of the Knights Templar, hence the name.

One of the oldest buildings still in use is the lonely little church at Bradwell called St. Peter's on the Wall. When the Saxon bishop landed near Bradwell much of the great 'Roman Fort of the Saxon Shore' was still standing; it must have been very like Houseteads. The

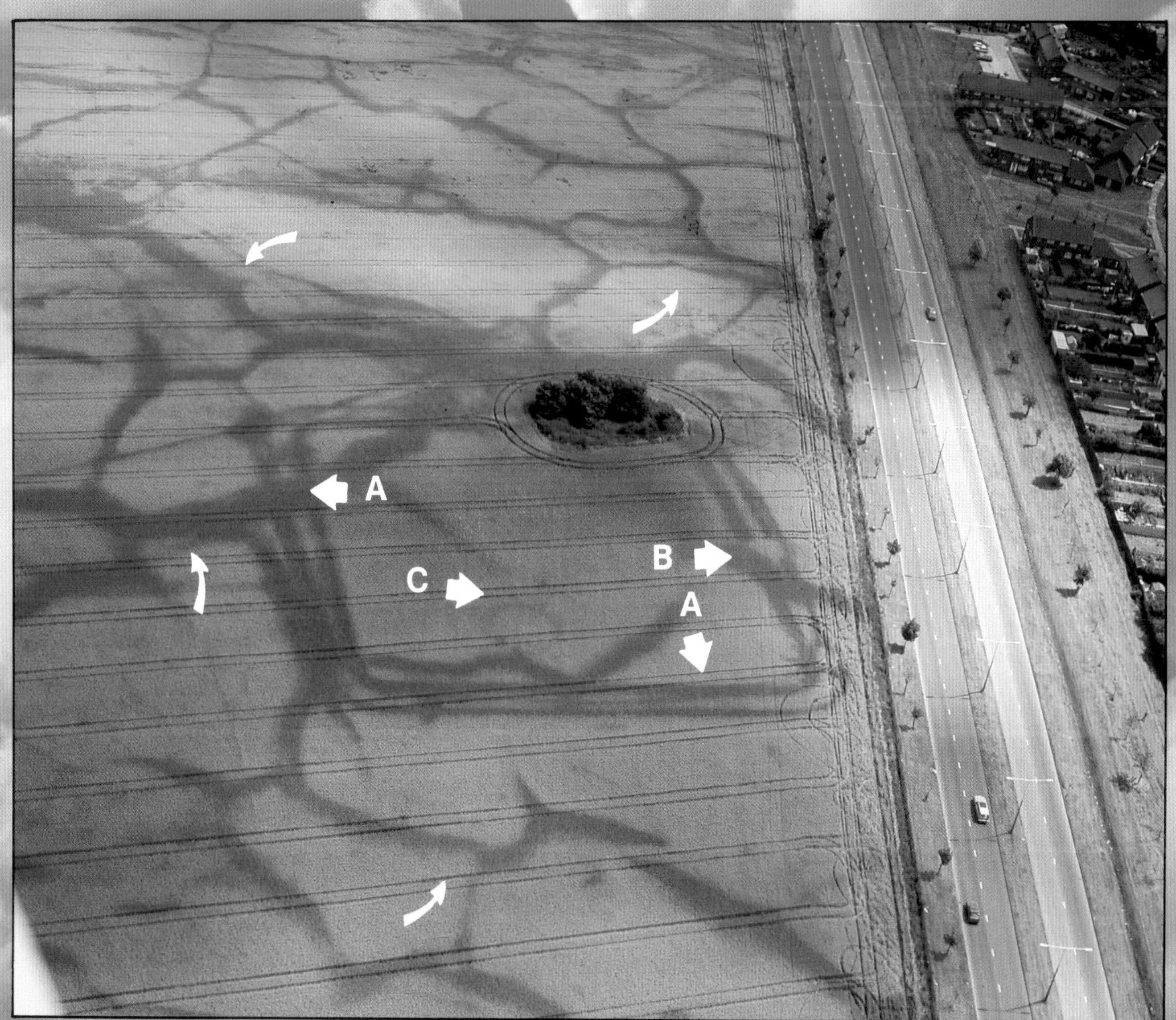

'Crop-mark of Later Bronze Age Camp (1200-700BC). The double enclosure is well defined (A), with entrance (B), and circular house (C). The irregular marks (arrowed) are 'ice-wedge polygons'.

year was 654 A.D. when St. Cedd, having sailed from Lindisfarne, landed in Essex. With materials from the fort he built his chapel astride its outer wall. Little now remains of the Roman fort 'Othona' apart from some stone, brick and tile in the chapel, a'crop-mark' of the wall in the adjacent field, and the name, St. Peter's on the Wall.

Saxon Church of St. Peter's on the Wall, Bradwell. Note 'crop-mark' of Roman Fort wall (arrowed). Inset: Roman red tile and other material incorporated in the walls of St. Peter's.

'Othona' the Roman Fort of the Saxon Shore, as it might have looked in the 4th Century AD. Painting by Peter Froste.

Near Hadleigh Castle a double rectangular mark shows most years; although when the field is planted with two different crops, usually only half the mark becomes evident. This fortified enclosure was built in the 'iron age' just before the Roman Period. At Thundersley the 'crop-mark', produced by stunted growth, is clear evidence of foundations beneath; this is the site of a Roman Villa. Another villa can be seen in the corn at Chignall, in this photograph the rooms of one wing show up as if 'drawn'. At Orsett a 'causewayed camp' of the Neolithic period (new stone age c.3000 B.C.), pre-dating Stonehenge is often visible. The causewayed camp was so called because the large circular banks and ditches which comprised it were not continuous, but interrupted with segments of undisturbed earth or causeways. The form of these camps is so distinctive that the marks could be nothing else. Near Manningtree by the River Stour the barrows (burial mounds) of a Bronze Age (c.1000 B.C.) cemetery show most summers.

Just south of Colchester, at Gosbeck's Farm is a massive Roman and Iron Age site in which is probably the most interesting feature is the crop-mark of a Romano-British Temple. The triple outer 'wall' can be clearly seen together with the much smaller double 'walls' of the temple. However, some years in place of the double inner 'walls' a vast single 'structure' with an entrance becomes manifest. This is evidence of an Iron Age temple which pre-dates the Romano-British Temple. There must be subtle differences in the soil and climate which determines which of the marks we will see. Very often the distinctive 'starfish' like shape of a decoy pond becomes visible, there were over thirty of these medieval duck traps around our rivers and coasts.

'Crop-mark' of Iron Age (just B.C.) building at Hadleigh.

Roman Villa at Thundersley.

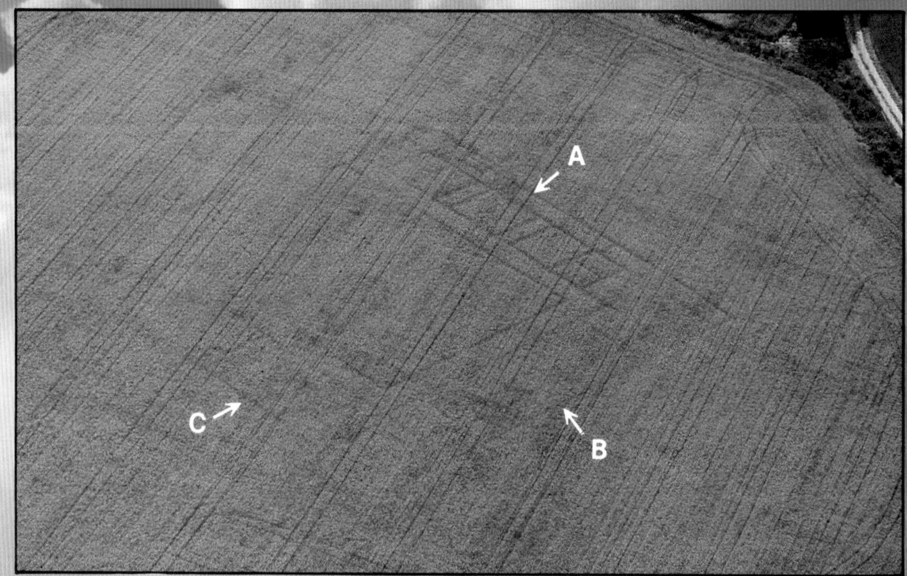

'Crop-mark' of Roman Villa at Chignall. The right wing and rooms show well (A), the front (B), and left wing (C) are less well defined.

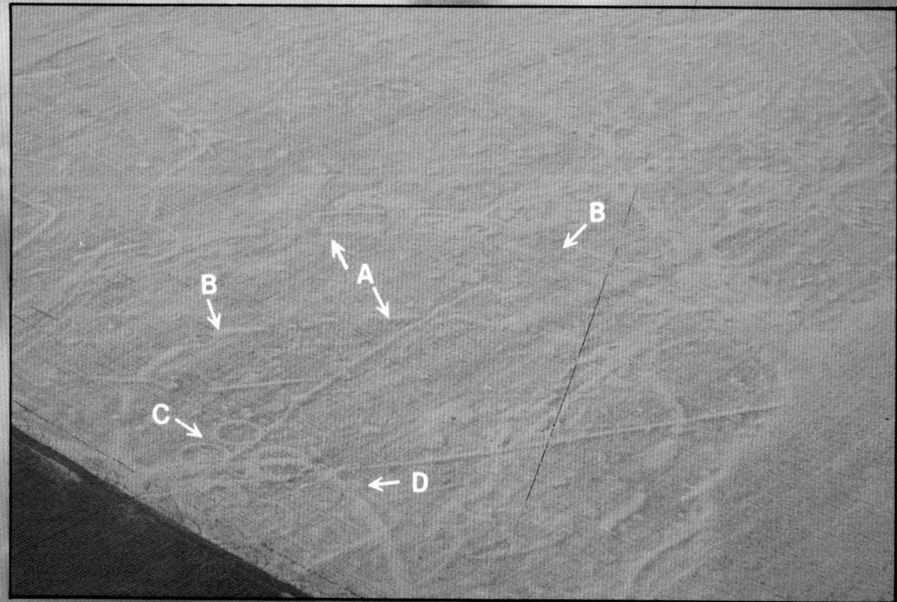

'Crop-mark' of Causewayed Camp of the Neolithic period, (new stone age about 3000 B.C.) Triple Causewayed enclosures show (A), with causeways (B). The circles (C), are probably barrows while the enclosure (D) which is superimposed, is clearly later.

'Crop-mark' of Romano-British Temple at Gosbeck's Farm near Colchester. The triple outer walls can be seen at (A) and the double inner walls of the temple (B).

'Crop-mark' of decoy pond at Bradwell. Note flattened crop.

'Crop-mark' of Bronze Age cemetery about 1000BC by the River Stour near Manningtree.

Sometimes at the Gosbeck's Farm site, this vast mark of an earlier Iron Age Temple appears instead of the double walls of the Romano-British Temple.

The riddle of the circles

Recent years have seen a vast media interest in 'crop-circles' increasing public awareness and with many of the theories concentrated on the supernatural. Most of these theories I would deny! However, one by-product of this publicity has been a spate of hoaxes, but these are usually easy to determine. These 'jokes' often have complex patterns with little relevance to the man made structures usually associated with 'crop-marks'. Often the path taken by the hoaxers can be seen in the crop from the field perimeter to the 'cosmic-circle', and often they use tracks left by farm vehicles.

The 'Cosmic Circles': An answer

Wiltshire and the west country where most of the 'circles' which have attracted media interest have been found is very rich in early history and so one would expect an abundance of 'crop-marks'.

Some observers have told how they have seen a strong wind create the 'circles' but the wind alone could not form such regular marks as it is too random. There has to be another factor!

Since 'crop-marks' are formed by the crop being of different height or colour than the surrounding crop it is reasonable to suggest that the crop forming the marks also has a different strength. Therefore strong wind and rain could flatten the weaker crop leaving the adjacent growth untouched.

This is reinforced by the pictures you see here for the two sites at Gosbeck's Farm and at Maldon, both revealed flattened crop after a night of wind and rain. While the very distinctive shape of the decoy pond, observed by chance, also formed with a crop flat to the ground.

Apart from the pranksters, it is the climate, the type of crop and other factors which influence the manifestation of 'crop-marks'. Because these factors are ever changing, observations in the future will reveal many, as yet, unknown sites; evidence of our rich but otherwise hidden heritage.

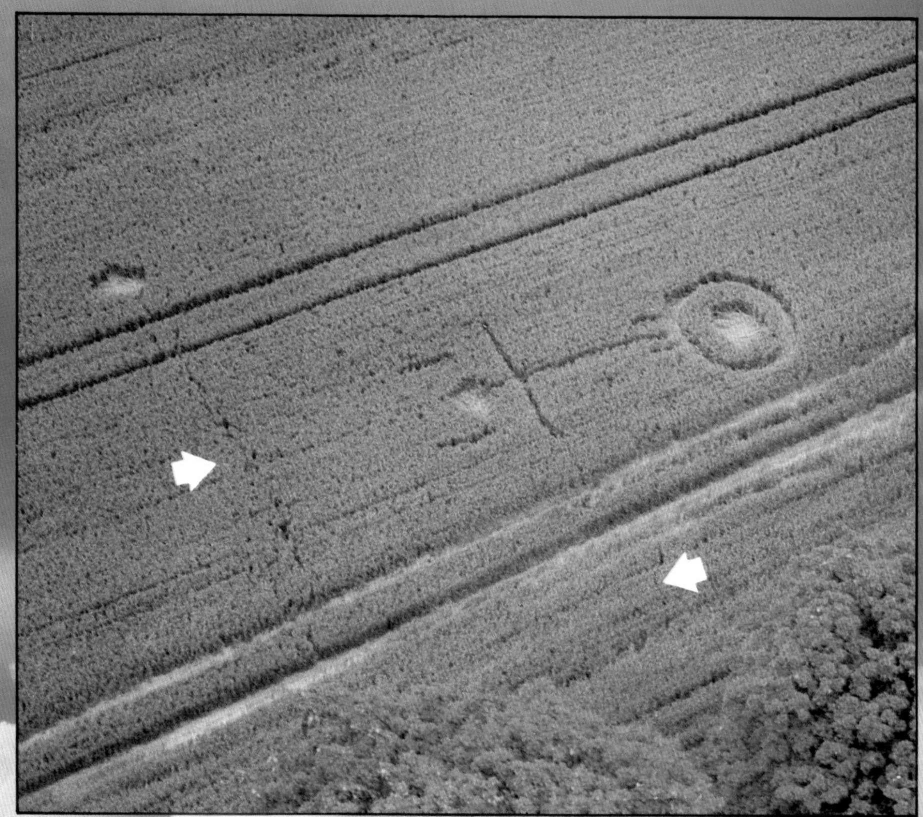

Hoax mark created near Southend Airport, probably made to make pilots 'bounce up and down', note paths of pranksters (arrowed).

The large mark of Iron Age temple at Gosbeck's Farm here the corn has been flattened by strong wind and rain.

The same mark, after the harvest, the corn of the mark has been flattened below the level of the surrounding stubble.

'Crop-mark' of enclosure and circular house near Maldon.

Same mark, but again the corn comprising the mark has been laid flat by strong wind and rain.

In the photograph above some of the Stanway squares can be seen and in the photograph below gravel extraction has already moved close to the site.

Just a few miles to the south west of Colchester and not too far from Gosbeck's Farm a series of five vast squares appearing most summers has given rise to much speculation. This site must have been one of the earliest discovered by aerial photography—the first observations were made in the nineteen thirties, and I have been watching the site with interest for about twenty years.

The five squares or enclosures are in two groups a series of three in line and another group of two.

Recently, the site by Stanway was scheduled to be used for the extraction of gravel and as a consequence would disappear forever. Colchester Archaelogical Trust set to work to excavate the squares working just ahead of the excavators.

Now, after several years of painstaking work some extraordinary finds have been revealed. The site had considerable importance about two thousand years ago when the area was used by the iron age peoples both before the Romans came and after the Roman conquest of Camulodunum *(Colchester).*

The earliest enclosures were probably first used for settlement or cattle but in the later part of the first century B.C. the largest of the enclosures came to be used for burials. Shortly after, the group of three enclosures was started, but unlike the other two these seem to have been constructed primarily for burials.

The largest of the burial chambers was in the centre of enclosure number 3, the only one of the enclosures with an entrance, which was in the centre of the eastern side.

This burial chamber was about the size of a small room, sunk about a metre into the ground, it had wooden walls secured with iron nails. The building had collapsed but the timbers were found in an orderly fashion some showing signs of fire. There were pottery fragments of some 24 pots, which must have indicated some wealth as they had all been imported from Gaul *(France)* and Italy. There was also a small quantity of cremated human bone. This is the largest known group of imported vessels of this period associated with a burial in Britain. It is clear that it was not a random selection of pots, but probably a dinner service buried with food, together with other goods like brooches, textiles, wood, leather and bone, alas these have all vanished without trace.

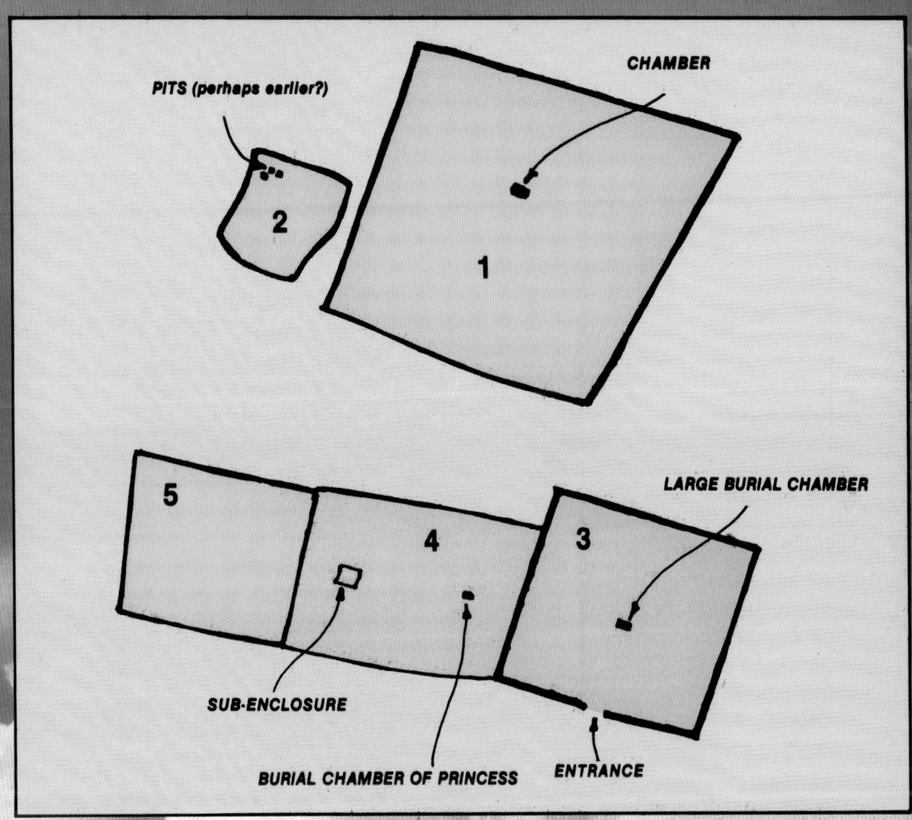

A diagram illustrating the form of the Stanway site, with the position of graves and entrance.

The enclosures (No. 3 on left and No. 4 on right) and the Royal Graves at Stanway on completion of excavation.

An artist's impression of how the site looked from the air during one of the cremations mid first century AD. Inset: Artist's impression of the Iron age priests and people placing goods in grave. Peter Froste.

The purpose of the chamber

There is evidence of a raised platform within the chamber and it seems likely there was a 'laying in state' with the body resting on the platform surrounded with the grave goods. The people would file past to pay their last respects then, homage done, the corpse was probably taken outside and cremated. Evidence of burning in the excavation suggests the funeral pyre was adjacent to the chamber, while the traces of metal found suggest some of the goods were burnt with the body. It seems the structure of the chamber was deliberately allowed to become part of the fire. The funeral and the feast which followed would have been grand, with vast numbers attending, the dead person was provided with a meal on the very pottery found. Later the bone from the cremation would have been carefully sorted from the ash and charcoal remaining from the the pyre. Then together with the pottery, which had been deliberately broken, the bone was placed in the chamber. Finally the burial was complete when the charred building collapsed and the chamber filled in. Possibly more earth was piled over the grave to form a barrow *(Burial Mound),* although these are rare in Britain from this period, there is one other in Colchester.

In the centre of the group of three enclosures *(Number 4),* was also the remains of a wooden chamber, both smaller and simpler than the other. Cremated bone was again found, together with smashed pottery which must once have been a large dinner service, with many of the pieces seeming to have been nested sets.

The glass phial of very thin glass, together with the remnants of a broken necklace also found suggest that this was the grave of a female and although perhaps not as important as the other burial, maybe she was a princess.

There is evidence of a number of other cremations on the site and other finds have been made including fragments of wooden and metal objects.

Grave goods with draught-like game.

Beautiful glass bowl probably from Italy.

Tear phial and brooch from grave of Princess

One of the jugs excavated from the grave.

The likely dates

It seems the earliest burials in enclosure 1, date around the end of the 1st century B.C. Next is the main chamber (enclosure 3) which was constructed around A.D. 20-30. It is almost certain that the female died after the Claudian conquest in A.D. 43, perhaps even as late as A.D. 80.

Who were they?

The graves must have been for important people of the Trinovantes, the Iron Age tribe which had control of the area with its capital Camulodunum, and it is likely that the occupants were related by marriage or birth. Cunobelin, a very great leader, held power until just after the start of the Roman invasion (A.D. 43), so the largest chamber, which is contemporary, was most likely for a close relative of Royal Blood who died whilst Cunobelin was 'King'.

The second chamber post dates the Boudican revolt (A.D. 60-61) and it is significant that it suggests the remains were of a person belonging to a tribe which did not side with Queen Boadicea, as the Romans otherwise would not have allowed such ceremonious burials. Cunobelin had a son Adminius who was instituted as leader by the Romans after the Claudian conquest of Camulodunum, it is almost certain that the lady was a close relative of the family, could it be she was a daughter and so a Princess of Britain?

Perhaps you could enjoy the thrill of discovering something new. There are a number of flying clubs in Essex and I am sure they would all welcome you for a flight into the past. The cost would not be too much and a flight over our Essex Countryside in late summer when an abundance of 'crop-marks' are to be seen could be a rewarding experience; and you might even have the thrill of shedding more light on 'Hidden Essex'.

The Decoys of Essex

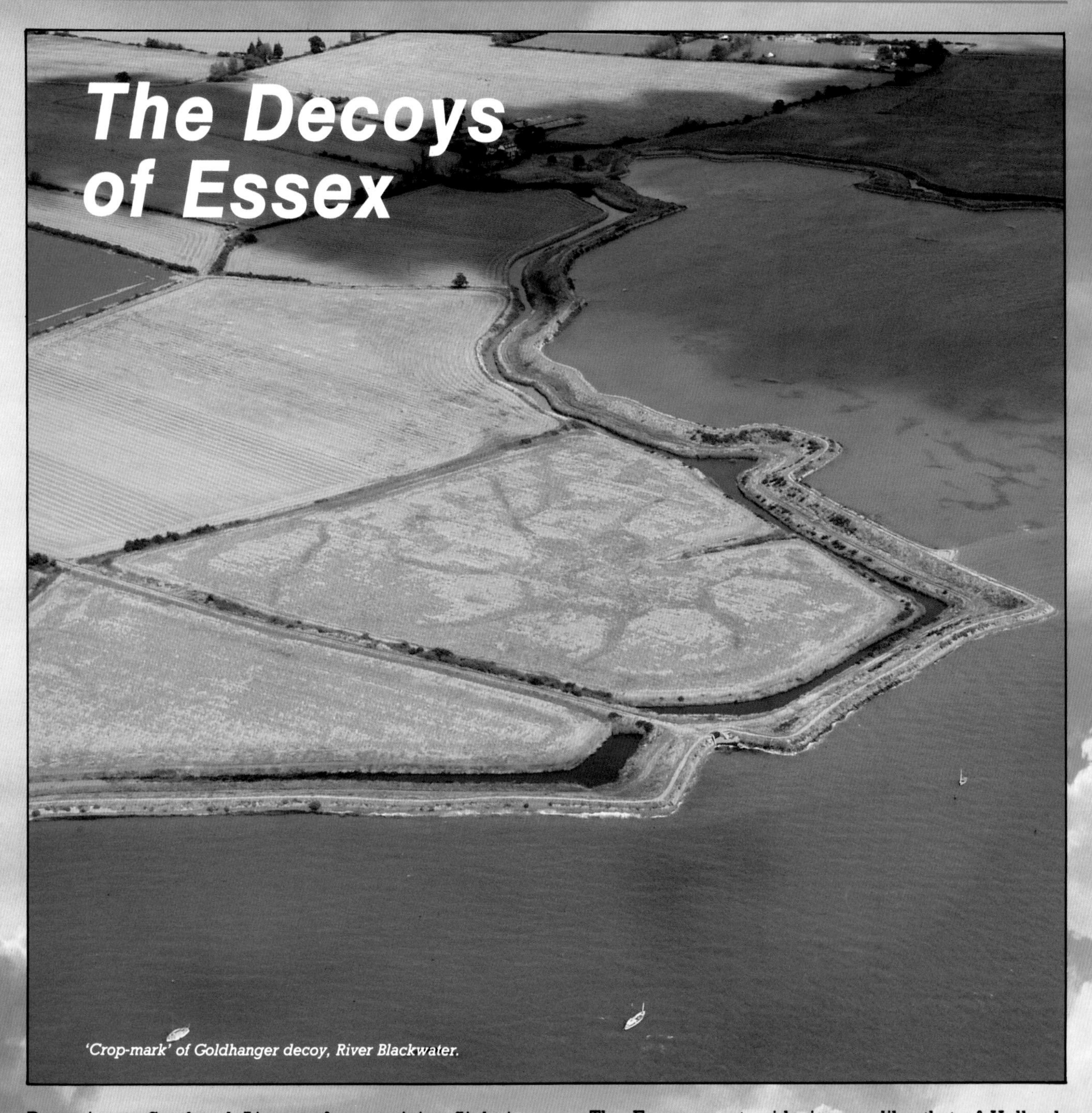

'Crop-mark' of Goldhanger decoy, River Blackwater.

Returning to Southend Airport after a training flight in the Clacton area of Essex, the River Roach was reflecting the evening sun and pointing the way to the airport and home. I relaxed briefly, enjoying the beauty of the sky, sea and rivers as the Cessna aircraft approached the River Blackwater, one of my favourite places. I was surprised when, on looking down there in a field was clearly to be seen a large dark patch with eight curved 'arms' extending out, each reminiscent of a cow's horn. The whole thing although huge, was like a starfish. I was looking down at the 'crop-mark' of Goldhanger Decoy Pond. *(Cropmarks are formed when earlier and usually otherwise invisible disturbances of the soil show in differences of growth in a crop grown above. They become visible mostly in the late spring when the crop is ripening through until the harvest and are best seen when flying above).*

Decoy ponds originated in the Netherlands where the Dutch name for was 'eene kooy' which translated means 'duck cage'. This name became changed in the English language to 'decoy' and in translation the meaning also subtly changed to that which we understand today.

The Essex countryside is very like that of Holland, with wide expanses of marshy ground fed with many broad shallow rivers and tidal inlets edged with saltings; ideal wildfowl habitat. Thousands of birds, mainly mallard, widgeon, teal and pochard accompanied by vast numbers of geese, enough to darken the sky, come in the autumn to these areas, especially during their winter migrations.

So the people of Essex and East Anglia copied the Dutch and built decoy ponds, I have discovered thirty one in Essex, many along the broad estuary of the River Blackwater. While others were constructed in Suffolk, Norfolk and Lincolnshire with more along the south coast, especially near the Chesil Beach at Abbotsbury.

The decoy ponds varied considerably in size and shape but they all had one thing in common, the large curved arms (called pipes) extending outwards. Where the pipes joined the pond their width was about 7 to 8 feet, narrowing and extending in a curve for about 150 feet. One of these 'pipes' depending on the wind direction would be covered for its length with a net, attached to semi-circular hoops to create a tunnel. A series of rush-plaited screens would be placed at judicious intervals and angles along one side to give cover for the 'decoy man' and his well trained dog.

Wildfowl were attracted in flight to the pond, sometimes by food put out by the wild-fowlers but, more often by tame ducks swimming around, although sometimes wooden 'decoy ducks' would be used. It is interesting to note that decoying wildfowl is not recent, 'decoy ducks' made of mud and feathers have been found in Egyptian tombs dating back about 4000 years. Once the ducks had alighted on the water, the dog, carefully chosen to have a fox like appearance and the same reddish-brown colour, would weave in and out of the screens. The ducks would follow; both out of curiosity and their natural desire to 'mob' the enemy, a fox! So the wildfowl finished in the narrow end of the 'pipe'; trapped!

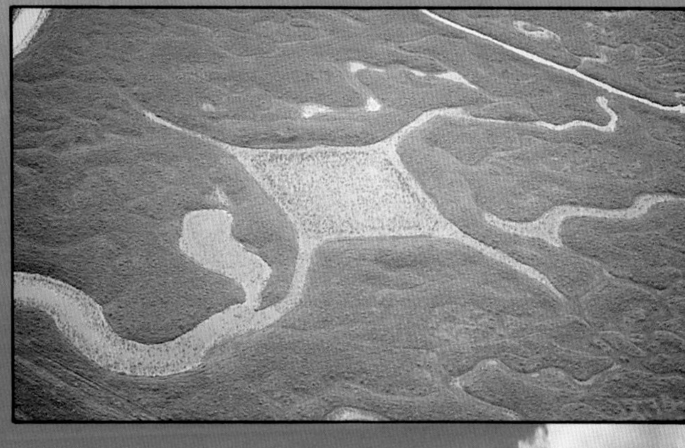

Remnants of decoy pond on Old Hall Marshes in the summer.

Remnants of decoy pond on Old Hall Marshes in winter.

A working decoy pond at Abbotsbury, Dorset. The netted 'pipe' can be seen on right.

Entrance to the 'pipe' of the Abbotsbury decoy, some of the rush screens can be seen.

Suitable ponds near the coast were turned into decoys from the late middle ages and used to trap wildfowl until recently, the late 18th century seeing the heyday. Considerable thought went into aiding nature in the construction of decoy ponds.

Willows were planted amidst beds or reeds and rushes, these provided both shelter for the birds and cover for the decoy men. An ideal day would be overcast with a light wind; the overcast sky would prevent shadows betraying the presence of the men and a light wind would cause the reeds to rustle and so mask the sound of the wildfowler's movement.

The large 'pipe' of the Abbotsbury decoy.

Large numbers of birds were trapped in this way, the Dutch claimed that in 1784 their coastal ponds netted 67,000. In Essex the Tillingham decoy trapped 3000 annually. Daniel's book 'Rural Sports' relates that the Reverend Bate Dudley captured 10,000 birds during 1799. In Goldhanger decoy, owned by Mr Buxton, Daniel reports that in 1802 "as many pochards (a diving duck) have been taken at one drop as filled a wagon, so as to require four stout horses to cart them away".

There is but one working pond in England today, at Abbotsbury in Dorset, where the decoy pond together with a swanery have existed since monasterial times. The decoy pond, together with the hooped nets over the pipe and rush-plaited screens, have been reconstructed to show a duck decoy as it must have looked in the 18th century, only now the wildfowl are ringed not slaughtered.

I find the old cliche 'it's a small world' still very relevant to me especially when flying, an occupation in which I spend most of my working days. I can walk into almost any airport and hear a call "hello Edward". So it was, on a recent cruise in the Indian Ocean that I came across another connection with the 'Decoys of Essex'. With a small party of 'explorers' I was aboard the M.V. Caledonian Star visiting some of the smaller islands. Sharing the voyage was Tricia Hardcastle. Tricia was talking of her home in Cornwall, a home she shares with a large number of animal and bird friends. During our conversation she mentioned 'calling ducks' some of

The 'pipe' of the Abbotsbury decoy on a perfect 'decoy day', overcast to prevent shadows from decoy men with a light wind to rustle the reeds and mask their noise.

Remnants of decoy on the Bradwell peninsular. Note how the area around the pond has been planted with trees and rushes to give cover.

which she has; my ears pricked up! It seems 'calling ducks' were bred in Holland to have an especially loud call to be used in their decoy ponds and so assist in the trapping of other ducks.

Many remants of decoy ponds can be seen today, however a short flight around the local coastline in the late spring or early summer would be needed to reveal the distinctive starfish like shapes which were once the 'Decoys of Essex'.

Very often I deliver illustrated talks on my flying adventures as the 'Spy In The Sky' usually the talks end with a question time, when the most often question I am asked is, "Don't you get fed up with flying above the fields of Essex?" The answer is always no, for I find every flight fascinating but when the opportunity arises to fly farther away I jump at it.

I have flown all over Europe in light aircraft, and often too, into North Africa, but probably my favourite place is the Channel Islands and especially Jersey.

The French Connection

One of the most famous places in Essex is Pleshey, a charming village with a perfect example of a Motte and Bailey Castle, the earliest type of defence built by the Normans soon after the defeat of Harold in 1066. However, the great castle was already in decay about 200 years before Shakespeare, for in Richard II, the Duchess of Gloucester asks of John of Gaunt that Edmond of York come to her.

> **Bid him-O, what?**
> **With all good speed at Plashy visit me.**
> **Alack, and what shall good York there see,**
> **But empty lodgings and unfinished walls'**
> **Unpeopled offices, untrodden stones?**

(Plashy is the old English word for Pleshey)

When my friend John Martinez telephoned and asked, "I have a spare seat in 'Yankee Hotel' (a 4 seat Cessna 172) to Jersey, would you like to come?" I jumped at the chance.

The departure from Southend was on a glorious morning and as the aircraft turned to the south west the River Thames was bright in the rising sun. Three ships were making a leisurely way towards London leaving triple 'herring bone' like waves which sparkled in the clear water.

John is a competent pilot so I was able to relax and enjoy the changing vistas of sea and sky. The aircraft levelled at 3000 feet and already I could see across Kent to Lydd, about 40 miles away and our first turning point on the coast. From there a turn towards the west took us across the channel. About halfway, and now at 8000 feet to the left was the Normandy coast of France, ahead the Contentin Peninsular and to the right the Isle of Wight, parts of Sussex and Hampshire. Even after many thousands of hours flying, such a seascape is still a moving experience. As we flew across the Contentin Peninsular I was in R.T. (radio telephony) contact with the controller at Brest, who, as we crossed the western coast of the Peninsular leaving French airspace handed us over to Jersey Radar. We were now cleared to descend towards the island clearly visible about 20 miles ahead. The approach to land was 'straight in' for runway 27 (runway 27 is 270 degrees from north, that is, landing in a westerly direction). Routing our Cessna across St. Helier, the whole length of the beautiful island over lush valleys with vast sunny beaches to the south and the rugged northern coast with its lovely bays to the north.

One big advantage of flying in a light aircraft is that the formalities are very brief and in about ten minutes we were exploring the island of Jersey in a hired car. We had an excellent lunch, returning to the airport in mid-afternoon. The day was still beautiful and the choice of route home was two fold. Either back across the sea after crossing the Contentin Peninsular again or turning to fly along the French coast, over Normandy, Dieppe, Le Touquet to Cap Gris Ney with a left turn to the radio beacon at Dover (a V.O.R.) across Kent, the Thames Estuary and so to Southend, home! John chose the latter and I was pleased.

We flew at only 1500 feet, outside controlled airspace with no requirement to speak to air traffic control, all was quiet peaceful and so beautiful as we crossed the beaches of Normandy, which in 1945 were in turmoil and carnage as the invasion progressed. Now, as I looked down, the sea was gently lapping the shore and what was left of the Mulberry harbour on the cliff top, starkly white, a military cemetery.

Remnants of World War II, mulberry harbour at Arromanches les-Bains, Normandy.

A little futher inland is Bayeux, 'The Cradle of the Dukes of Normandy'. A city still dominated by its magnificent Gothic Cathedral, dedicated to Our Lady (Notre-Dame), the towers date from the time the original building was completed in 1077. As we circled the city enjoying the splendid view of the Cathedral lighted by a soft setting sun, my thoughts went to another invasion, that of William Duke of Normandy and of Pleshey, a tiny village north west of Chelmsford in Essex.

William sailed on the 27th September 1066, landed at Pevensey and just to the North of Hastings at a site now called Battle, defeated Harold and his Saxon army. By modern standards the battle was quite small, with only about 8000 warriors on each side. The armies first made contact in the morning and by dusk William's victory was complete.

The Cathedral of Our Lady (Notre Dame) Bayeux, Normandy.

Although the numbers were few and the duration short, the repercussions were momentous, changing the history of this England and possibly that of the world.

We enjoyed the rest of the flight, we turned at Cap Gris Nez for the Dover beacon (a radio navigation aid for aircraft) crossed Kent and had a superb view of Canterbury Cathedral, of Leeds Castle touched by the low July sun, and of the north downs beyond, landing at Southend just as the sun was setting with a row of war birds lined up on the apron.

William the Conqueror as the Duke came to be called, left his mark indelibly on Essex. If you look at a map, about 10 miles north west of Chelmsford is the village of Pleshey and printed by its name is the legend 'Castle'. The word usually suggests a mighty stone keep like the one at Castle Hedingham. So often visitors to Pleshey are disappointed to find only earth works, a mound, together with an enclosure surrounded with an earth bank. The whole vast complex is encircled by a moat, it is a 'Motte-and-Bailey Castle' the Motte being the mound, while the enclosure is the Bailey. Pleshey is a magnificent example of this earliest type of Norman Castle.

Cap Griz Nez and the English Channel.

Battle Abbey, Sussex. Site of the Battle of Hastings. The Saxons occupied the daffodil covered bank in front of the Abbey.

Pleshey Motte and Bailey Castle (12th century). The bridge which spans the moat dates from the 15th century.

Artists impression of how Pleshey looked in its heyday between 1250-1350AD. Peter Froste.

Castle Hedingham. The very fine keep on its 'motte' (a mound) rises almost 100 feet above the Essex countryside.

The Manor of Pleshey was granted by the Conqueror to Eustace, Earl of Boulogne and subsequently it came into the possession of Geoffrey de Mandeville who began the Castle in the mid twelfth century.

The main village street was once a Roman road, the Motte lies to the south of this street and rises fifty feet above the countryside dominating the village, adjacent to the Motte is the Bailey, a vast courtyard area. The earth taken to build the mound and the banks which surround the Bailey, created the moat which surrounds them both. The original Norman fort would have been a stout wooden tower surrounded by a stockade at the summit of the Motte, the Bailey would have contained all the ancillary buildings.

Most Norman castles began their life in this way, but later evolved into the massive stone keeps and surrounding wall we more usually visualise when we think of a 'castle', yet even so, in most Norman castles the Motte-and-Bailey concept can be clearly seen.

Canterbury Cathedral, touched by a late afternoon sun.

Leeds Castle and the North Downs of Kent.

The Bayeux Tapestry, depicting the building of a great earthwork like Pleshey.

'Warbirds' at Southend Airport.

At Pleshey, a bridge connects the Bailey to the Motte, this bridge spans the moat in one graceful arch, it dates at least from the fifteenth century and is probably the oldest brick built bridge in Europe. The view from the summit of the Motte is most rewarding, with much unspoiled typical Essex countryside visible all round. Set out like a map, the village, with the defensive bank and ditch which has encircled and contained Pleshey from ancient times,is clearly to be seen.

The Cathedral of Our Lady at Bayeux once housed the Bayeux Tapestry (it is now on view in the William Conqueror Centre at Bayeux). The Tapestry gives a graphic account of the events leading up to, and of the Norman Conquest, the connection with Pleshey is an illustration of the building of a great earthwork very like the Pleshey Motte-and-Bailey Castle.

There were a number of such castles in Essex, Rayleigh, Ongar, Orsett and Castle Camps to name but a few.

Pleshey, with its fine Motte-and-Bailey Castle is best viewed from a light aircraft, about one thousand feet above, however an earth bound visit has additional rewards. A walk around the ancient streets and defences is like stepping back in time, many of the houses are decked with flowers, while in the spring the banks and ditches are resplendent with primroses.

Bayeux in France has its magnificent Gothic Cathedral of Our Lady, Pleshey, a typical Parish Church dedicated to the Holy Trinity. Bayeux is quite large, Pleshey tiny, but the Bayeux Tapestry and the Pleshey Motte-and-Bailey Castle complete the French connection.

Essex Wildlife Trust

Two Tree Island and Brent Geese

While flying above the Essex Wildlife Trust reserves can be very rewarding and yield excellent photographs, many of the sites are sensitive, so pilots must be careful not to disturb the residents. Of course also the flyer is unable to observe the abundance of interesting flora and fauna which are available to the ground based visitor, when beautiful photographs can be made of the flowers and the hides used to take pictures of the birds.

The Essex Naturalists' Trust was founded in 1959 for the purpose of nature conservation, to acquire and maintain some of the wonderful wildlife sites in which Essex, with its very rich coasts and tidal estuaries abound. A great landmark for the Trust came in 1961 when it was able to purchase a worked out sand and gravel quarry known as Freshwater Pit situated on the banks of the River Colne. This became the Trust's first wholly owned nature reserve, and from then it reverted to its historical name, Fingringhoe Wick.

This place probably encapsulates the history of Essex, for as the climate, following the retreat of the ice age about 12,000 years ago, became warmer so the fauna evolved as the permaforest wastes gave way to birch woods. Then pine, followed by oak woodland which flourished for centuries. During these changes ran a thread of human activity from the Palaeolithic (stone age) hunter to the Neolithic (new stone age 4500-2000 B.C.) forest clearer, then came Bronze age settler to be followed by Iron age farmer, these later to be conquered by the Romans. When the Romans left Essex and Fingringhoe in the 4th Century A.D. there were Saxon Villages, then in medieaval times the serfs inhabited Fingringhoe. During the wool boom of the 19th century sheep grazed by the river and in the 20th century gravel workers toiled until they exhausted then abandoned their quarries. Soon after that the trust took over Fingringhoe Wick. Now, after much hard work the lovingly restored site is visited by members of the Trust and the public who can now enjoy the wonders of our Essex countryside.

This vignette of life at Fingringhoe Wick is typical of life in many places in Essex, especially by the broad shallow rivers of which there are plenty.

Buttercup Meadow, Warley Place.

Fingringhoe Wick, on the River Colne.

Fingringhoe Wick, headquarters of the Essex Wildlife Trust.

This now superb reserve covers 125 acres, it has three nature trails with a leaflet for each describing the places of special interest to be found along the trails and these places are identified by numbers, one of the trails is suitable for the disabled. There are eight bird hides, some fronting the saltings of the River Colne, and an Observation Centre with information and a shop. The wide range of habitats in the reserve attracts many birds and mammals, so that the woods are filled with birdsong, even the nightingale can be heard, there are over twenty breeding pairs there.

Flint tools of stone age man have been found at Fingrinhoe where he once hunted beaver bison and elk. In Roman times, pelicans and cranes fished on the shallow marshlands where now you can see kingfishers and tawny owls, the winter is an especially good time to observe a wide range of wildfowl and waders which migrate there.

New Reserves

Fingringhoe is rather special, but the Trust has now ownership or management of 77 sites with a total of over 4600 acres a remarkable achievement, but it does not stop there, the management are always on the lookout for new sites to acquire for the benefit of us all.

One of the most recent is an area of 143 acres of coastal grazing marsh and saltings on the River Crouch, opposite Burnham. A sanctuary for overwintering birds such as brent geese, wigeon, teal, pintail and curlew. This new reserve Lower Raypits was opened in June 1992 by the Lord Lieutenant of Essex Admiral Sir Andrew Lewis, Patron of the Trust.

The name— Essex Wildlife Trust

You will have noticed that I used the original title of the trust earlier 'The Essex Naturalists Trust. A few years ago the name was changed to The Essex Wildlife Trust and I for one was pleased. During the years I have presented many illustrated talks mainly about our country from the air and especially Essex. Our countryside and conservation is something I have tried to promote but when I spoke of the Essex Naturalists Trust, eyebrows went up and I am sure my audience visualised the members tripping nude about the woodland clearings and on the beaches; however the vision was shortlived when the slides were projected.

Lions Creek and Lower Raypits, the new nature reserve for the Rochford and Southend Area. Lions Creek is the small enclosed area of water while Lower Raypits abuts the River Crouch.

Grays Chalk Quarry.

Swans on the Abberton Reservoir.

Abberton Reservoir

Situated to the south of Colchester is a great man-made lake, Abberton Reservoir. Here the people of Essex have a vast and most important wildlife sanctuary on their doorstep. Winter is probably the best time to enjoy the incredible spectacle of thousands of birds feeding in and around the water. However any time is beautiful, there are of course ducks, swans and geese on the water, and, in the trees a large colony of cormorants nest. By the waters edge one can enjoy watching terns, wagtails and sandpipers to name but a few; a truly wonderful wildlife experience, and just a few miles from home.

To make it easy, the Trust has created a visitor centre by the waters edge. There you can sit in comfort by the panoramic window and observe the sights. Then perhaps finish your visit with a purchase from the shop in the centre which specialises in wildlife books, binoculars and gifts. Such a purchase will help the Trust in its continuing work.

Abberton Reservoir, the Conservation Centre.

Two Tree Island

Two Tree Island is just off the coast opposite the famous cockle sheds at Leigh-on-Sea, and it is possible to view the masses of wildfowl from the Peter Boat, a pub in Old Leigh, while enjoying a drink and a dish of cockles.

The reserve was once a refuse tip, when that ceased, an interesting flora developed in the soils which were brought to cover the rubbish. Many unusual plants flourish there together with numerous small mammals and insects who have made it their home. As a consequence, kestrels can often be seen hunting overhead and sometimes a short eared owl, unusual gulls too, can often be seen.

However, it is the adjacent mudflat and saltmarsh, the best surviving in the Thames Estuary, on which grows an abundance of eel grass in dense beds (zostera noltii and zostera augustifolia), the principal food of the dark-bellied brent geese. When autumn comes to the Thames Estuary, vast flocks of brent geese leave their summer home in Siberia to overwinter in the gentle climate of Essex and feed on the eel grass by Two Tree Island. People who live nearby say "you can set a clock by the arrival of the geese".

Two Tree Island and Leigh-on-Sea, low tide and the wide expanse of eel grass, the brent geese fly so far to feed on, can be seen.

Two Tree Island, snow covered.

Warley Place

Standing on high ground just to the south of Brentwood is Warley Place. On a clear day the tall buildings of London stand out on the skyline to the west, and to the south one looks across the Thames to the Downs of Kent. The gardens were laid out by the diarist John Evelyn between 1649 and 1655 but probably reached their heyday during the life of the last occupant of the house and gardens, Miss Willmott. She remodelled the gardens and introduced to them a vast number of plants from all over the world. Miss Willmott was one of the great horticulturalists of all time. She owned gardens in both Italy and France as well as Warley, where she employed over a hundred gardeners.

The house was demolished in 1939 following a lonely Miss Willmotts death on 27th September 1934, and the gardens went into decay. The story did not end with her death and the destruction of the house, for in 1977 Warley Place was leased to The Essex Naturalists Trust and since then the members of the Brentwood and Billericay group of the Trust have strived to restore it, at least in part, to its former glory.

Warley Place is best visited in the spring when it is a glory of spring flowers. The reserve is bordered by the well known Crocus Field. In the early spring, the field is a sea of purple as the Early English Crocus bursts into bloom. The field is one of the few sites in Britain where this crocus grows naturally, records date this miracle back to the 16th century. However, the present abundance is due in part to Miss Willmott who had her gardeners scatter seed. When the crocuses fade their purple gives way to the brilliant yellows of masses of daffodils which are prolific, as they are also in the undulating meadow to the south. This meadow is best viewed from the reserve, with a magnificent vista across the daffodils to the city buildings and spires of London.

Open day at Warley Place, the daffodil walk.

Warley Place in Winter.

Miss Willmott was able to look through this door across the lawns of Warley Place towards London.

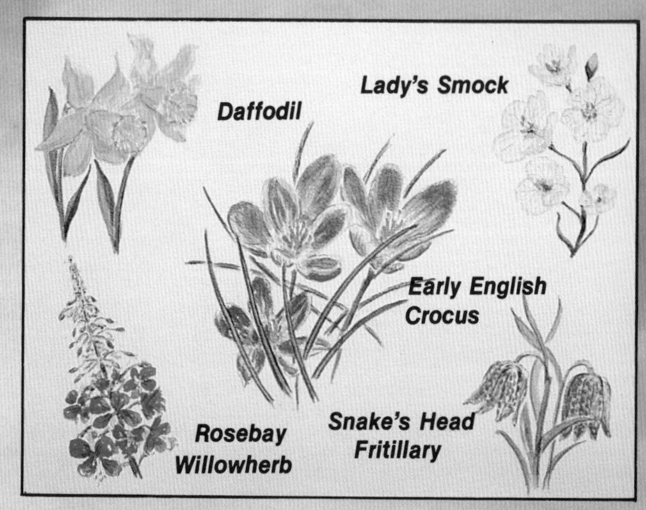

Some flowers of Warley Place.

A bird hide overlooks the surviving area of lakes which are known to have existed in Saxon times and later were carp fish ponds for Barking Abbey.

Such was the fame of Ellen Willmott during her life that something over fifty flowers, plants and trees have been named for her or Warley.

A descriptive Guide to the Nature Trail Exists with the places of plants, trees and features of special interest, numbered. There you can walk amongst the flowers, shrubs and trees far too numerous to name here, because Ellen Willmott was a great collector, some of the plants are exotic. As the undergrowth is opened up by the members of the trust who were helped by the great storm of 1987 more light gets through and life comes again to many plants which have laid dormant beneath the soil.

Other Reserves

Many of the reserves are quite tiny, often dedicated to preserving one rare species or particular habitat, while many are of national and even international importance. Quite a number of the reserves have open days when members of the public are encouraged to visit, the timing of these open days usually coincides with the most important feature of the reserve. Look in the local paper and listen to the local radio for dates, such a visit can be a great joy!

The Essex Wildlife Trust is a charity which welcomes new members. The annual subscription is quite modest and for it you can visit many of their wonderful reserves, help with the conservation projects and see the efforts you make, returned in tangible form in the preservation of otherwise irreplaceable parts of Essex.

Warley Place, the daffodil walk.

Roman River Valley, inset early purple orchid.

Aerial Photography? —Try It!

Contrary to popular belief, to get into the air with your camera is probably much easier than you could imagine and much less costly than you might expect.

Beagle Pup, 'Juliet India' above the stratus cloud layer.

The Flying Club

Your first requirement will be an aircraft. With nine flying clubs operating about one hundred aircraft from six airfields in the county, there must be an aircraft available for photography near your home. *(Within the British Isles as a whole there are about 130 flying clubs, almost every large city or town has one),* operating about 750 aircraft). Having been a Chief Flying Instructor at Southend Airport for over 20 years, I can assure you that most flying clubs will welcome you for a photographic flight, as we do a Southend. Usually this would mean joining the club but this should not present a problem as most flying organisations have temporary membership at modest cost.

The Aircraft

The high wing Cessna aircraft is the type most used for training and recreational flying, so this is the aircraft you are most likely to be offered.

Fortunately this is the aircraft most suitable for air photography. The high wing provides an excellent field of view, while on each side of the cabin a large window opens out and up in flight, so avoiding the impediment of shooting through perspex. The Cessna is also able to fly both slowly and safely.

The Camera

There is no need for a special camera to produce superb air-to-ground or air-to-air shots, any modern 35mm camera is capable of excellent results.

Most people unininitiated to air photography tend to think that a long focal length lens is required, this is not so. I find most of the time I use a standard lens and when a longer focal length is required seldom have need of a lens longer than 135mm, while on some occasions I even resort to a wide angle lens. Since camera shake, as in most photography, is the most significant problem, when conditions permit I set the shutter at 1000th of a second or more, only using a slower speed if necessary to achieve the correct exposure. Having set the shutter speed the aperture will, if the camera is automatic, adjust to the correct setting, otherwise the adjustment must be made manually to give the correct exposure for the available light. Because the subject is always at 'infinity', depth of field is not a consideration, so the wider apertures associated with the high shutter speeds are acceptable.

Again, with the subject always at 'infinity' there is no need to focus the camera, so, I hold the camera in such a way as to keep the lens against the infinity stop. For the most part air photography depends on crisp sharp pictures, therefore a clear bright day is essential. Any hint of mist or haze will degrade the images and should be avoided; except for those odd occasions when a light mist will produce an evocative result.

Choice of Film

When shooting in good weather, which is best, medium speed film is quite fast enough. I usually use Ilford FP4 at 125 ISO for black and white, Ektacolour Gold at 160 ISO for colour negative and Ektachrome 100 exposed at 160 ISO (to increase colour saturation) for my transparency requirements. Recently I have been using Fuji Vélvia when conditions have permitted, it is a slow film 50 ISO, but the results have been excellent. I only use a higher speed film when the weather is poor and the shot is a 'must'.

Hadrian's Wall and Housesteads Roman Fort, Northumberland.

Other Requirements

Of course there are some legal requirements to be considered. If the photography is commissioned it is regarded as a commercial operation with the requirement that the flight must be conducted by a commercial pilot. That is a pilot licensed to receive payment for his flying. However, if the pictures are for your own use or for a freelance project, a commercial pilot, private pilot or flying instructor may conduct the flight, (now all flying instructors also hold commercial pilot's licences).

An aircraft is not permitted to fly closer to people, buildings, structures, vessels, etc. than 500 feet; while over built up areas not lower than 1500 feet or at a height at which it could glide clear in the event of an engine failure. This means that over large towns and cities it is necessary to use a multi-engined aircraft or a helicopter, this of course is much more costly. A multi-engined fixed wing aircraft is on average two to three times the cost of a single, and a helicopter four to seven times as much. Unless one has a particular requirement to photograph a subject in built up area it is best avoided. There are an unlimited number of interesting subjects to photograph while flying over the open countryside, above rivers and by the sea; when a single engined aircraft may be used.

In certain controlled airspace, London for instance, prior permission is required and a special flight number is issued to facilitate liaison with air traffic control. The 'non standard flight number' as it is called, is made valid for a certain time, often a month, but always with enough time to take account of the variables especially the weather, aircraft availability, etc. Broadly speaking the airspace in this country is divided into two sections, controlled, where advanced permission is usually required and uncontrolled airspace where, apart from obeying the basic low flying rules, no permission is required. The flying club you have chosen to fly from will be able to advise you on these matters.

Rievaulx Abbey, Cistercian 12th century, North Yorkshire.

Changing the Guard, Buckingham Palace, London.

Over London!

Most of my flying over London has been in a twin engined Piper Apache aircraft with the rear window removed. I cannot expect to convey in words the thrill of flying at a relatively low level (usually between 1000 and 1500 feet) over a great city like London, especially at dusk.

One day, just by chance, while on a photographic detail I found myself looking down on Buckingham Palace, it was a beautiful summer morning and there below the visitors were enjoying that very British spectacle, The Changing of the Guard.

A Chance Scoop!

My flying duties as an instructor have presented me with many opportunities for air photography; as when I have been about those duties I often put my camera on board, just in case! On one such occasion as I was flying back from Newcastle on Tyne over Yorkshire and looking down saw the very lovely ruins of the Cistercian Abbey of Rievaulx, it looked glorious in the late afternoon sun.

Trafalgar Square.

Every photographer dreams of a scoop! Like most scoops, mine came purely by chance. I had taken off from Southend Airport in a Piper Apache twin engined aircraft to conduct an air test as the machine had just completed an overhaul. The test was required before the re-issue of its Certificate of Airworthiness. 'Mike-Uniform' (that was the Apache's call sign) was delivered late from the hanger and as I flew northward from Southend the sun was lowering in the west.

The test should have taken about an hour and a half to complete, but very early in the flight a fault became apparent which necessitated my return to base. As I approached the airport I could see a huge column of smoke to the seaward. The reason for the smoke was not immediately apparent although there was obviously a big fire. I quickly landed, gathered my camera, another aircraft with a pilot and was soon airborne again; in time to see Southend Pier at the height of the blaze which destroyed it. That evening I was fortunate enough to achieve the only air to ground pictures of that awe inspiring sight and they were reproduced in most of the nations newspapers the following day.

Southend Pier Fire, July 29th, 1976.

Sometimes Deliberate, Sometimes Chance

Sometimes I set out on a flight with a particular shot in mind. So it was on Christmas Eve that with clearances complete I took off from Southend Airport in the 'Apache' at dusk, for London, to photograph St. Paul's and Trafalgar Square at night. We arrived over the city a little early, as the sun was setting. The City as always was a magnificent sight, however the ambient light was not as low as I wanted so we circled looking down, the office lights appeared to get brighter as the daylight faded. The thousands of people below must have been making their last Christmas greetings as they prepared to leave their offices for the stations and home. At last the light was as I wanted, we turned west towards St. Paul's and made a couple of orbits around the floodlit Cathedral before continuing past the South Bank with its theatres.

We flew along the River Thames which was spanned with 'necklaces' of lights which were the bridges. Following the river as far as Westminster Bridge and the Palace of Westminster where we turned north and soon there below was Trafalgar Square, crowded with people and dominated by the sparkling Christmas tree.

One lovely September evening I flew to Chatham to photograph a 'Parade of Sail'. There were 100 tall ships taking part, making a magnificent sight as they sailed down the River Medway on that soft September evening. It was such a beautiful flight that I was reluctant to return to base, so I turned south and saw the last rays of that evening sun caressing Rochester Cathedral before returning to Southend Airport.

A day of fair weather with cumulous clouds peppering the sky can be super for air photography, just as it is for ground work. It was such a day in September this year when in a Citabria aircraft with a local pilot I lifted off from an ex RAF airfield in Northumberland to photograph some of the glories of the heritage coast. With great castles, picturesque towns, Holy Island, Lindisfarne and then, just a short time away in an aircraft, Hadrian's Wall.

A day like this lends itself to excellent pictures but when the shadow of a cloud is on the subject to photograph, the light becomes very flat and lifeless so it becomes necessary to circle, carefully watching the shadows of the clouds as they move across the ground until once again the subject is lighted by the sun, then quickly back in for the shots. Sometimes my flying takes me further afield, the great cathedral at Florence was taken during a refuelling stop on the way to Naples.

St Pauls Cathedral, London. Floodlit on Christmas Eve.

Airborne Camera Technique

A good technique for using a camera in an aircraft is to have the aircraft's speed reduced to slow safe, then put the aircraft into a gentle descending turn. Shooting through an open window you can observe the changing light and shoot when the subject looks best. The latter part of the day is my favourite time, when the sun is lowering, the shadows long, and the light soft.

A Glory, a well named natural phenomena, the circular 'rainbow' forms round the shadow of the aircraft when the shadow falls on a light cloud cover.

A mist January morning, here fog has formed mainly over the colder rivers Crouch and Roach. The line through the sky is an inversion. In an inversion the temperature of the air above is warmer than the air below so the fog and haze stay trapped near the ground.

London in 1934 taken from 5500 feet. Notice in those days how St. Paul's Cathedral dominated the City. The South Bank was undeveloped with the Shot Tower still standing. Then barges and ships came upriver as far as Westminster Bridge.

Wembley Arena.

Tower Bridge, London, with a Sandringham flying boat moored nearby.

London from Wapping. *St. Katharine's Haven and the Tower of London can be seen by Tower Bridge, just beyond is HMS Belfast, on the right is The Embankment while past that are The Palace of Westminster and Buckingham Palace.*

The City of London.

HMS Ark Royal is saluted as she is moored in The River Thames at Greenwich.

Canary Wharf, Millwall.

Above: *Amerigo Vespucci. Full rigged ship, salutes the Royal Naval College, Greenwich, Amerigo Vespucci is the Italian sail training ship. She is named for the great Italian explorer and it is after him America is named.*

Left: *The German Barque Gooch Foch (231 feet) sets sail from Falmouth for Lisbon.*

'Farewell to London', R.R.S. Discovery passes under Tower Bridge on a ship carrying ship after 50 years, on her way back to Dundee where she was built. This ship took Captain Scott to the South Pole in 1911. (R.R.S.—Royal Research Ship).

The London Zoo, Regent's Park.

Above: *St. Katharine's Dock c1965. To the right of the picture is the Royal Mint while on the South Bank a power station is still working. Wharfs and shipping extend beyond Tower Bridge.*

Below: *St. Katharine's Haven, now much changed but the Ivory House in the centre of the Haven has been preserved.*

15th century Hampton Court Palace.

Kew Gardens

The Palace of Westminster, Big Ben and Westminster Abbey.

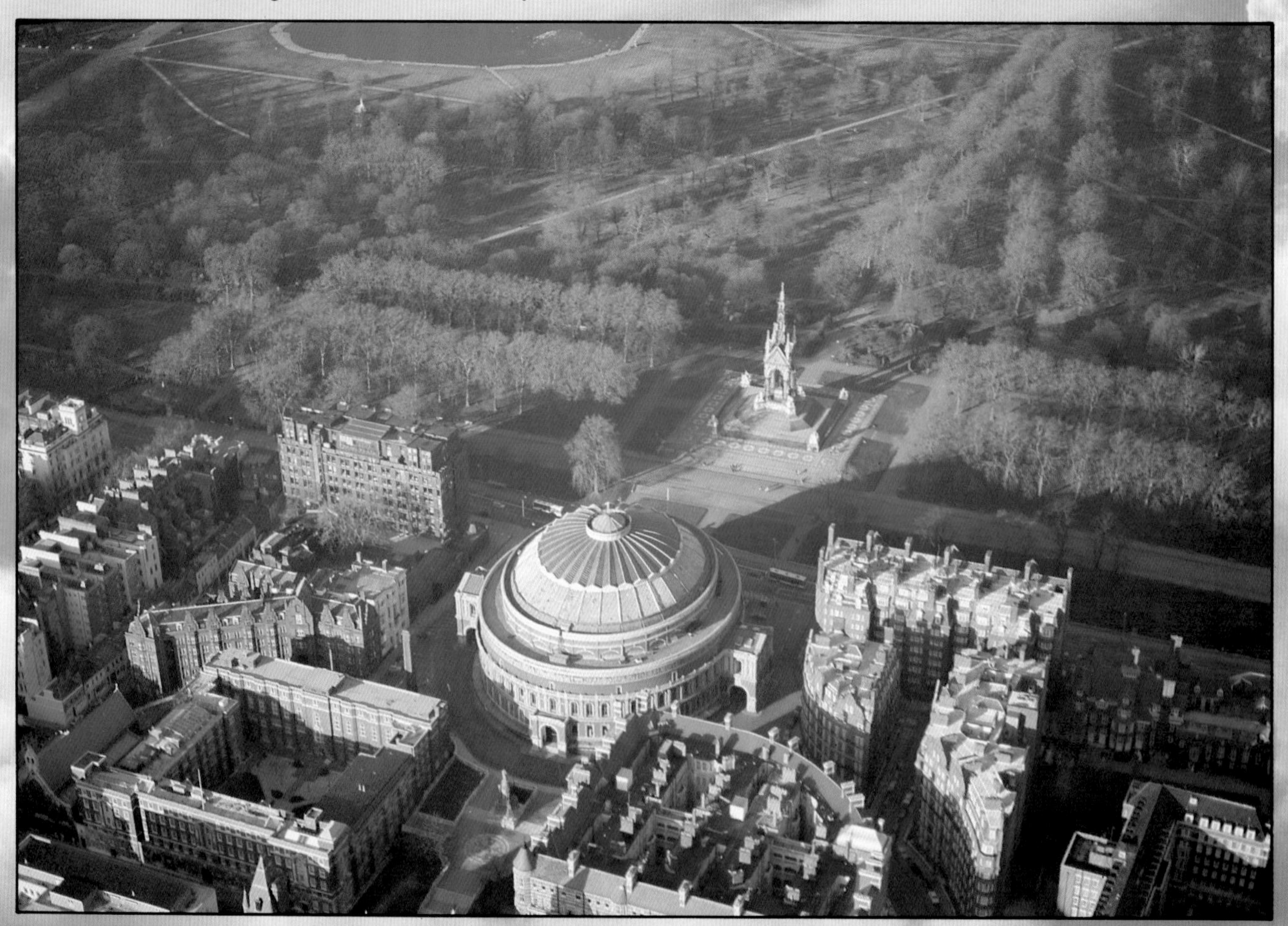

The Albert Hall and the Albert Memorial, Hyde Park London.

The White Cliffs of Dover, often a visitor's first sight of England.

Rochester Cathedral and Rochester Castle touched by a setting September Sun.

'Parade of Sail' on the River Medway.

Hever Castle, early 15th century and the girlhood home of Anne Boleyn the tragic Queen of King Henry VIII.

Leeds Castle, Kent, said by Lord Conway to be "The most beautiful castle in the world".

Holy Island and Lindisfarne, Northumberland. It was from here that, at the request of Sigbert, King of Essex, St. Cedd sailed to Bradwell, founded his community and built St. Peter's-On-The-Wall.

Trafalgar Square, Christmas Eve.

Now Take To The Air. . .

Now, hopefully, having wetted your appetite to get into the air and put this new dimension into your photography I am sure you will like to know a little about the likely costs. A single engined aircraft like the Cessna 150 or 152 with a pilot/instructor will cost about £80 per hour, but prices vary a good deal due to the differing costs of operating at various airfields. This sounds quite a large sum but in truth a great deal of country can be covered in an hour and a fair number of sites photographed. Like so many things some time spent in thought and preparation is well worth while.

Plot your subjects on a good map. I usually use an Ordnance Survey map. Be at the flying club early enough to spend some time with your pilot before the flight. The other day for instance, I photographed nine great houses along the Weald of Kent in just fifty minutes. Hever Castle was amongst them, looking very lovely with the trees resplendant in their new spring colours and the lawns yellow with daffodils. I hope these words and pictures have encouraged you to get into the air to enjoy the experience of flying in a light aircraft coupled with your love of photography. Enjoy your flight!